Scottish Mythology

Enthralling Myths, Folktales, and Legends from Scotland

© Copyright 2024 - All rights reserved.

The content contained within this book may not be reproduced, duplicated, or transmitted without direct written permission from the author or the publisher.

Under no circumstances will any blame or legal responsibility be held against the publisher, or author, for any damages, reparation, or monetary loss due to the information contained within this book, either directly or indirectly.

Legal Notice:

This book is copyright protected. It is only for personal use. You cannot amend, distribute, sell, use, quote, or paraphrase any part, or the content within this book, without the consent of the author or publisher.

Disclaimer Notice:

Please note the information contained within this document is for educational and entertainment purposes only. All effort has been executed to present accurate, up-to-date, reliable, and complete information. No warranties of any kind are declared or implied. Readers acknowledge that the author is not engaging in the rendering of legal, financial, medical, or professional advice. The content within this book has been derived from various sources. Please consult a licensed professional before attempting any techniques outlined in this book.

By reading this document, the reader agrees that under no circumstances is the author responsible for any losses, direct or indirect, that are incurred as a result of the use of the information contained within this document, including, but not limited to, errors, omissions, or inaccuracies.

Free limited time bonus

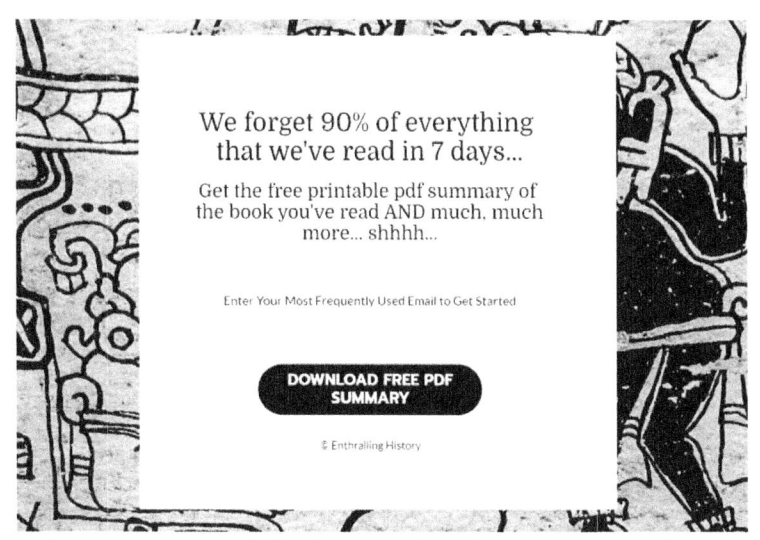

We forget 90% of everything that we've read in 7 days...

Get the free printable pdf summary of the book you've read AND much, much more... shhhh...

Enter Your Most Frequently Used Email to Get Started

DOWNLOAD FREE PDF SUMMARY

© Enthralling History

Stop for a moment. We have a free bonus set up for you. The problem is this: we forget 90% of everything that we read after 7 days. Crazy fact, right? Here's the solution: we've created a printable, 1-page pdf summary for this book that you're reading now. All you have to do to get your free pdf summary is to go to the following website: https://livetolearn.lpages.co/enthrallinghistory/

Or, Scan the QR code!

Once you do, it will be intuitive. Enjoy, and thank you!

Table of Contents

INTRODUCTION 1
CHAPTER 1: THE BEGINNING: CREATION MYTHS AND THE SCOTTISH LANDSCAPE 4
CHAPTER 2: LEGENDARY HEROES AND WARRIORS 14
CHAPTER 3: DEITIES AND SPIRITS: THE PANTHEON OF SCOTTISH MYTHOLOGY 26
CHAPTER 4: THE FAE AND THE UNDERWORLD: DIFFERENT REALMS 37
CHAPTER 5: GHOSTS AND APPARITIONS 47
CHAPTER 6: THE MYSTERIOUS CREATURES OF SCOTTISH FOLKLORE 59
CHAPTER 7: WITCHCRAFT, DARK MAGIC, AND CURSES 71
CHAPTER 8: LOVE AND BETRAYAL: THE SAGAS OF SCOTLAND ...82
CHAPTER 9: SACRED SITES 90
CONCLUSION 101
HERE'S ANOTHER BOOK BY ENTHRALLING HISTORY THAT YOU MIGHT LIKE 104
FREE LIMITED TIME BONUS 105
BIBLIOGRAPHY 106

Introduction

Scottish mythology is deeply rooted in Celtic mythology, sharing common threads with its Irish counterpart while also possessing unique elements. Historically speaking, the Celts originated in central Europe during the Late Bronze Age, around 1200 BCE. They were not a unified nation but rather a collection of tribes sharing linguistic, cultural, and social similarities. Their society was characterized by a rich oral tradition, skilled craftsmanship, and a complex religious system with druids as spiritual leaders.

Over time, the Celts began to expand their territory. However, their migration was not a single, coordinated movement; instead, it was a series of waves that spanned several centuries. These migrations were driven by various factors, including the need for more space due to booming populations, the allure of trade, and perhaps the search for lands suitable for farming. By the Iron Age, around 800 BCE, Celtic tribes had spread across a large part of western Europe, even reaching Britain and Ireland.

The Celts' arrival in Scotland is pieced together from archaeological findings and historical deductions, as there are no written records from the Celts themselves during that time. It is believed they arrived in Scotland sometime during the last few centuries before the Common Era began. What we can be sure of, however, is that their arrival marked significant cultural shifts, with the local people of Scotland starting to adopt Celtic languages, artistic styles, and social systems.

As the Celts settled in Scotland, their myths and legends became deeply rooted in the Scottish landscape. The gods, heroes, and mythical creatures of Celtic lore were adapted to the Scottish environment, embodying the features of its mountains, forests, and lochs. The natural world was central to Celtic spirituality, and this connection is vividly reflected in Scottish mythology.

The spread of Celtic influence in Scotland was not just cultural but also linguistic. The Celtic languages, part of the Indo-European language family, diversified into several branches, with Gaelic becoming dominant in Scotland. This language carried with it the stories, poems, and songs that formed the backbone of Celtic mythology.

It's important to note that the Celtic influence in Scotland was not a case of cultural replacement but one of integration and synthesis. The existing beliefs and traditions of Scotland's indigenous populations melded with those of the Celts, creating a unique cultural and mythological identity.

In Scottish mythology, you find unique entities like the Kelpie, a shape-shifting water spirit, and the Cailleach, an ancient hag representing the harshness of winter. These figures, while uniquely Scottish, echo the broader Celtic fascination with nature and its spirits.

The similarities with Irish myths are also seen in shared characters and motifs. For instance, the Irish hero Fionn mac Cumhaill appears in Scottish tales too, albeit with variations. Likewise, the concept of the Otherworld, a mystical realm inhabited by deities and the dead, is prominent in both mythologies.

Both Scottish and Irish myths emphasize the power of storytelling and oral tradition. These stories were passed down through the generations and were more than just entertainment; they were a way of understanding the world and conveying social and moral lessons.

For example, the tragic love tale of Deirdre and Naoise is one of the most popular tales that has been passed down through the ages. It has themes of love, freedom, and destiny, all of which resonate deeply in both Scottish and Irish folklore, illustrating the often-tragic nature of love and the cruel twists of fate. In contrast, the tale of Thomas Rhymer and the Queen of Elfland offers a different perspective. Thomas Rhymer, a bard known for his prophetic talents, encounters the Queen of Elfland, a mystical figure from the Otherworld. She invites him to her realm, where he stays for seven years. Unlike Deirdre and Naoise's story, this tale is not marked by tragedy but rather by enchantment and mystery.

Witchcraft, dark magic, and ghostly apparitions also hold a prominent place in the rich fabric of old Scottish beliefs. In Scottish folklore, witchcraft was often viewed with a mixture of fear and awe, with witches depicted as possessing powerful abilities. The late 16th and early 17th centuries witnessed intense witch hunts, reflecting societal fears and religious influences.

Ghosts in Scottish lore, on the other hand, are frequently tied to specific locations like castles and ancient sites. Tales of restless spirits often serve as moral lessons about the consequences of one's actions. Similarly, curses in Scottish myths are seen as powerful forces capable of bringing misfortune, underscoring the belief in the power of words and spells.

In short, the origin of the Celts in central Europe and their gradual migration to Scotland brought about a rich cultural heritage. The migration of the Celts to Scotland is a story of cultural blending, where old tales were reshaped and evolved, resonating across the highlands and lochs and shaping the very soul of Scottish mythology.

Chapter 1: The Beginning: Creation Myths and the Scottish Landscape

In the far north of Europe, where ancient mountains rise like silent guardians and lochs lie deep and mysterious, lies Scotland. Its rugged beauty, carved over millennia, tells a story older than time. To understand its formation, we must first embark on a journey back to the Ice Age. It was a time when great sheets of ice as thick as mountains covered the land. These glaciers moved slowly but sculpted the valleys and hills, leaving behind a landscape both harsh and breathtaking.

However, there is another tale, one woven into the very fabric of Scottish folklore, about the shaping of this land. It speaks of the Cailleach, also known as Beira, the ancient hag and the creator and shaper of mountains and valleys. Her story is one of magic and mystery, an intricate blend of the harsh realities of nature and the rich imagination of the ancient peoples.

The Cailleach was no ordinary figure. She was the embodiment of winter and the land's wild, untamed nature. Her appearance was as formidable as the elements she controlled. She was often depicted as a giantess, towering over the landscape, her skin as pale as snow and as rough as the rugged mountainsides. Her eyes, piercing and blue, mirrored the icy lochs and the winter sky. Her hair, long and white, flowed like the cascading waterfalls, and her voice was like the howling wind.

A 1917 illustration of the Cailleach.
https://commons.wikimedia.org/wiki/File:Wonder_tales_from_Scottish_myth_and_legend_(1917)_(14566397697).jpg

  With a hammer made of thunder and lightning, the Cailleach roamed the land, sculpting its features. One legend explains how Scotland turned into the rugged landscape that we see today. The Cailleach roamed the lands of Scotland with a large creel, or wicker basket, filled with rocks and stones. These weren't ordinary rocks; they were the building blocks of the land itself, charged with the magic and might of this ancient deity. As she traversed the rugged terrain, her task was to create and shape the features of the land, such as its mountains, hills, and valleys.

However, as she journeyed across Scotland, occasionally, either through carelessness or due to the sheer weight of her burden, rocks fell from her basket. Each rock, which was imbued with her power, transformed into a part of the landscape. Where a large stone fell, a mountain would rise, rugged and majestic. Smaller stones formed hills, and the smallest pebbles became boulders and crags.

This process, repeated over time, led to the formation of Scotland's unique and varied topography. This story elegantly blends the idea of an accidental yet fateful creation with the deliberate shaping of the land. It paints the Cailleach not only as a creator but also as an elemental force whose actions, whether intentional or not, have profound impacts on the natural world.

The Cailleach was also the powerful being that was responsible for the creation of Scotland's very first loch. According to folktales, there was a magical well on top of Ben Cruachan, a mountain. Each night, the divine hag had to cap the well to prevent it from overflowing, and each morning, she removed the cap so that the water could flow. However, on one fateful night, the Cailleach accidentally skipped her routine. Perhaps exhausted by her daily labors, the hag fell into a deep sleep, forgetting to cover the well.

The water from the well began to flow unchecked the entire night. It gushed forth in torrents, cascading down the mountainside with unstoppable force. By the time the Cailleach rose from her slumber, the water had formed an immense loch in the valley below. This great body of water became known as Loch Awe.

The revered hag goddess of winter also played a pivotal role in the changing of the seasons. As autumn's colors faded and winter's chill began to whisper across the valleys, the Cailleach was said to move to the Gulf of Corryvreckan. Here, amidst the roaring waters, she washed her immense great plaid, a significant task that ushered in the transformation of autumn's twilight into winter's deep embrace.

Legend has it that Corryvreckan, with its fierce and swirling currents, became her washtub. The whirlpool, known for its thunderous roar, is a permanent feature of the landscape. Although the whirlpool is always present, its visibility and intensity vary with the tides. Some claim the sound could reach distances as far as twenty miles away and lasted for three full days.

The Corryvreckan whirlpool, believed to be the Cailleach's washtub.
Walter Baxter / The Corryvreckan Whirlpool:
https://commons.wikimedia.org/wiki/File:The_Corryvreckan_Whirlpool_-_geograph-2404815-by-Walter-Baxter.jpg

Once done, the great plaid would be pure white, as it had been thoroughly cleansed in the churning waters. This cloth, transformed by the old goddess's hands, then became the expansive blanket of snow that gently covered the land.

The Cailleach was more than just a creator; she was a guardian of animals and a protector of the wild. She nurtured the deer and the wild goats, and her presence was felt in the rustling of leaves and the whispering of the wind. Her persona was complex. She could be fierce and formidable, like the storms of winter, but she could also be nurturing and protective, like a mother to the land and its creatures.

Legends say that the Cailleach would transform into a beautiful young woman once every hundred years, but she would age rapidly as the seasons turned. This cycle symbolized the eternal rhythm of nature, the never-ending dance of creation and destruction, life and death, and winter and spring.

A Battle between Two Giants: Benandonner and Finn McCool

Benandonner, known as the Red Man of Antrim, was a being of immense size and power. His home was among the towering cliffs and deep valleys of Scotland, a land as hard and unyielding as the giant himself. Legends of his strength and valor were as common as the heather on the hillsides.

Across the narrow sea lay Ireland, home to another giant, Finn McCool. Although Benandonner had never met Finn, he had heard tales of his Irish counterpart. Finn McCool, also known in Gaelic as Fionn mac Cumhaill, was not just any giant. He was a warrior, a leader, and a man of great wisdom and bravery. His feats were the stuff of legend, and his valor was celebrated in the Celts' fireside tales.

The tale we are recounting began in Ireland, where Finn, standing on the rugged cliffs, would often gaze across the North Channel toward Scotland, wondering about the giant he had heard of but never seen. Finn, whose pride was as great as his stature, grew restless with the thought of another giant who might match or even surpass his strength. Although Finn was said to have lived peacefully with his wife Oonagh, Benandonner's continuous taunts shouted from across the sea eventually led to Finn's fury.

Every day, the two giants exchanged insults, both shouting at the top of their lungs. Eventually, they began to hurl rocks at each other. However, their throws were not powerful enough; the distance between them was too vast. Finn once threw a lump of land toward Scotland, but it fell short. Landing in the middle of the ocean, this great lump of land formed the Isle of Man. The location from where the lump of land was collected was filled with water, becoming what we know today as Lough Neagh.

There was no sign that the rivalry between the two would cool down. Perhaps driven by a desire to prove himself the greatest giant in the land and to teach the mysterious Scottish giant a lesson for taunting him, Finn finally decided to challenge Benandonner to a face-to-face battle. But there was one problem that stopped him from doing so: the vicious sea that lay between them. However, Finn was never known to back down. Days later, the undeterred giant eventually came up with an idea. He collected his strength and began to pick up huge chunks of the Irish coast and throw them into the roaring sea. These stones formed a causeway that stretched all the way to Scotland.

Meanwhile, in Scotland, Benandonner saw this path forming and understood Finn's challenge. Burning with his own pride and the fire of competition, Benandonner started his journey across the causeway toward Ireland, eager to meet Finn in battle. This was the exact moment when Finn finally understood the humongous size of Benandonner; the Scottish giant was way larger than him. Benandonner's stomp on the causeway could shake the very ocean that separated their lands. For the first time in his life, Finn felt a touch of fear.

Finn rushed to his dwelling, where his dearest wife, Oonagh, was waiting for him. In an almost trembling voice, Finn told his wife about Benandonner and his fearsome size. The Irish giant was terrified of his fate, as he was confident that it would be nearly impossible to defeat Benandonner in battle. Thankfully, Oonagh was renowned for her beauty and her cunning mind. Upon listening to her husband's worry, the giantess quickly devised a plan and chose to use cunning to outwit brute strength. First, Oonagh dressed Finn as a baby, swaddling him in an enormous blanket and placing him in a massive cradle. The disguise had to be convincing; Benandonner was no fool.

When Benandonner arrived in front of their door, Oonagh welcomed him with warmth. She explained that Finn was out on an errand but would return shortly. As they waited, she gestured toward the cradle, introducing the disguised Finn as their baby. Benandonner was surprised when he saw the huge infant.

"If this was the size of their baby, how big could the father be?" Benandonner thought to himself. The sight of the "baby" was definitely intended to sow a seed of doubt in Benandonner's mind about the size and strength of his rival. However, this was not enough to send the Scottish giant back to where he came from.

So, Oonagh went on with her plan. She offered him an oatmeal cake, a common treat in those parts. But this was no ordinary cake. Oonagh had cunningly baked a large iron griddle into the center of the cake. When the unsuspecting Benandonner bit into it, he let out a roar of pain as his tooth shattered against the hidden metal.

She had also presented a soft, griddle-free cake to the "baby" Finn. The disguised giant easily bit into it, exacerbating the illusion of the child's strength. Benandonner watched in astonishment and growing trepidation as the "infant" munched happily on the cake, a task Benandonner had found painfully impossible. Again, his mind raced with thoughts of how formidable Finn must be if his child possessed such strength.

But Oonagh wasn't finished yet. She handed a "rock," which was, in fact, a lump of soft cheese, to the disguised Finn, casually mentioning how Finn had taught their son to squeeze juice from a stone. Finn squeezed the cheese, making it appear as if he was extracting liquid from a rock.

Benandonner was intrigued. He attempted to replicate the feat with a real rock. He let out deep grunts as he strained and struggled, yet no juice came forth. The implications were clear to the Scottish giant. If a mere infant could perform such a feat, what kind of monstrous strength did his father, Finn McCool, possess?

Convinced that he could not win a duel against such a formidable rival, Benandonner excused himself, his pride overshadowed by a newfound respect and fear. He hurried back to Scotland, and while doing so, he desperately dismantled the causeway behind him, eager to put distance between himself and the mighty Finn. The remnants of that causeway, now known as the Giant's Causeway in Ireland and Fingal's Cave in Scotland, are said to be proof of this legendary encounter.

The Giant's Causeway, Northern Ireland.
code poet on Flickr., CC BY-SA 2.0 <https://creativecommons.org/licenses/by-sa/2.0>, via Wikimedia Commons: https://commons.wikimedia.org/wiki/File:Causeway-code_poet-1.jpg

Fingal's Cave, Scotland.
https://commons.wikimedia.org/wiki/File:Scotland-Staffa-Fingals-Cave-1900.jpg

The Isle of Skye

The Isle of Skye is yet another treasure trove for Scottish myths and legends. With its rugged cliffs, the Isle of Skye is a land where the boundary between reality and legend blurs. Among its many enthralling tales, the story of the Old Man of Storr stands tall—quite literally—as one of the isle's most captivating legends. There are a few tales that tell the story of this magnificent and towering rock formation. The shortest tale tells us that this striking pinnacle is the remains of a giant. Centuries ago, the isle was said to have been a home for giants. However, war constantly raged across the land, and during one particular battle, an unnamed giant fell on the Trotternish Peninsula. For unknown reasons, his body was abandoned, but instead of the body decaying, the land swallowed it up, leaving only one part of the giant protruding from the ground. While some say the Old Man of Storr was the fallen giant's thumb, others suggest it was a rather more intimate part of his lower body.

The Old Man of Storr, Isle of Skye.
Diliff, CC BY-SA 3.0 <https://creativecommons.org/licenses/by-sa/3.0>, via Wikimedia Commons: https://commons.wikimedia.org/wiki/File:Old_Man_of_Storr,_Isle_of_Skye,_Scotland_-_Diliff.jpg

Another story attributes the mystical landscape of Skye to the isle's mischievous fairies. The tale revolves around a local couple known for their devotion to each other. Every day, without fail, they climbed the hills of Skye and sat there, witnessing the beauty that Mother Nature holds. However, as the years turned to decades, the couple aged, and the climb grew more challenging. Eventually, the wife, with her strength waning, could no longer make the journey. Her husband, on the other hand, was steadfast in their tradition. Without complaint, he carried her on his back, determined to keep their ritual alive.

As more time passed, even the husband's strength began to dwindle, but his resolve never wavered. The mysterious fairies of Skye, having observed this display of love and tenacity, were moved and intrigued. They appeared before the couple, offering to grant the husband's silent wish that his wife could accompany him wherever he went.

With a heart full of love and hope, the husband carried his wife up the hill one last time. Upon reaching the summit, the fairies, true to their word but not without their own brand of mischief, transformed the couple into a massive stone pillar. United in stone, the couple would forever be together, an eternal symbol of love and dedication.

Not all of Skye's tales are tinged with the fairies' trickery. One such story is of a kind-hearted farmer who lived at the foot of these same mystical slopes. This farmer, known for his generosity and good nature, one day happened upon a Brownie in distress. Brownies, according to Scottish lore, are benevolent household spirits known to aid in domestic tasks under the cover of night. In this particular tale, the Brownie appeared to be injured. So, without hesitation, the farmer offered shelter and care.

Grateful for the farmer's kindness, the Brownie promised to repay his benevolence. True to its word, the Brownie became the farmer's unseen helper. Night after night, the farmer awoke to find his chores completed and his fields tended to with great precision and care.

The farmer's fortunes grew, as did his gratitude toward his unseen helper. Since he did not wish for free labor, the farmer often left out small tokens of appreciation, such as bowls of fresh cream or freshly baked bread, all of which would be gone by morning. Their friendship grew closer each year until tragedy hit.

The farmer was engulfed with sadness when his beloved wife suddenly passed away after battling a terminal disease. His heart shattered to pieces, and he was so heartbroken that he died the next day. The Brownie was devastated upon hearing news of its dear friend's death. In a display of appreciation and honor, the creature carved out a memorial to forever remember the kind-hearted farmer, creating the world-famous Old Man of Storr.

Chapter 2: Legendary Heroes and Warriors

Much like the epic tales of Herakles in Greek mythology or the heroic deeds of Aeneas in Roman lore, Scottish legends of heroes like William Wallace and Robert the Bruce resonate deeply with the ethos of their people. These stories, rich in not only drama but also moral lessons, served as a guide for the Scots, who had to wade through some pretty turbulent periods in history. These characters, born from a blend of history and myth, have transcended their mortal origins to become symbols of national pride. Their stories are far more than mere entertainment; they are the bedrock upon which the Scottish nation has been shaped and defined.

Sir William Wallace is a popular national hero of Scotland. His story, set against the backdrop of English domination over Scottish lands, is a saga of resistance, valor, and sacrifice. The late 13th and early 14th centuries saw Scotland under increasing pressure from the English Crown, which sought to assert control over its northern neighbor. This period of political turmoil and unrest laid the foundation for Wallace's emergence as a pivotal figure in Scotland's struggle for freedom.

Stained glass featuring a depiction of Sir William Wallace.
Otter, CC BY-SA 3.0 <http://creativecommons.org/licenses/by-sa/3.0/>, via Wikimedia Commons: https://commons.wikimedia.org/wiki/File:Wallace_Monument_20080505_Stained_glass_William_Wallace.jpg

Born around 1270, Wallace grew up in Scotland, where the shadow of English rule loomed large. His early life, shrouded in the mists of time, is a blend of fact and folklore. It is believed that he was the son of a Scottish landowner, possibly a minor noble. His youth was marked by a growing resentment against presence and influence of the English in Scotland.

The flame of rebellion was ignited in Wallace's heart when he witnessed a series of injustices. The spark that set his path ablaze was an encounter with English soldiers in the town of Lanark. There are few details about the incident, but according to legend, Wallace was incensed by the unjust killing of his beloved, Marion Braidfute. He retaliated by killing William Heselrig, the English sheriff of the town. This act of defiance marked the beginning of Wallace's legendary resistance against English rule.

His exceptional leadership skills and military acumen shone even brighter on the morning of September 11th, 1297. Standing atop a high hill, William Wallace looked out over the River Forth, his eyes blazing with the fire of impending battle. Those who saw his presence at the time likely thought that he was a striking figure, full of energy and charisma, and that he was more than prepared for the upcoming bloodshed. Below him was the narrow wooden Stirling Bridge stretching across the river; this was the location where one of Scotland's most famous fights would take place.

When the time drew near, Wallace eyed the movement of his enemies on the other side of the battlefield. Next to him were his loyal Scottish troops, a diverse group including farmers, blacksmiths, and some lower-ranking nobles lined up in a somewhat disorganized formation. Their eyes, filled with a mix of fear and determination, were all trained on their leader, awaiting his command. Wallace's army was outmatched in numbers and equipment, but their strong resilience and spirit would drive them to achieve success.

The Stirling Bridge today.
https://commons.wikimedia.org/wiki/File:Stirling_Bridge.jpg

On the other side, one could witness a sea of English soldiers, led by the earl of Surrey and Hugh de Cressingham, making an advance. The troops were filled with well-equipped knights and soldiers, were well versed in vicious battles, and were so used to winning that they thought the Scots to be nothing but mere disturbances. As they approached the bridge, one could hear the loud sounds of their armor clanking, their horses neighing continuously, and the piercing shouts of English soldiers. They were confident they would emerge victorious that day. Little did they know they were heading straight into a trap.

As the first units of the English army began to cross the narrow bridge, Wallace's strategic genius became apparent. He had allowed just enough of the enemy to cross, creating a bottleneck. With a thunderous roar that seemed to shake the very earth, Wallace led his men in a ferocious charge. The Scots, fueled by a fervent desire for freedom, descended upon the trapped English with a ferocity that belied their humble origins.

The narrow bridge became a scene of chaos, the clash of steel on steel resounding along the waterfront. Wallace wielded his sword with lethal grace, cutting down English soldiers with each swing. His fellow Scots, emboldened by their leader's valor, fought with a wild, untamed ferocity, their battle cries merging with the sounds of battle to create a symphony of carnage.

As more English troops tried to cross the bridge, the congestion turned their advance into a death march. The Scottish forces seized the opportunity and pushed back with renewed vigor. The river, once a serene ribbon of blue, turned crimson with the blood of fallen soldiers.

Amidst the chaos, Wallace stood as a symbol of indomitable will. His presence on the battlefield was electrifying. He inspired his men to feats of bravery that would have seemed impossible. Under his leadership, the Scots turned the tide against their oppressors, transforming their disadvantage into a weapon. As the battle reached its climax, the English were completely thrown into disarray. Sensing victory, the Scots pressed harder, driving their enemies back across the bridge.

In the aftermath, as the sun set over a battlefield strewn with the dead and dying, Wallace stood triumphant, his sword dripping with the blood of his foes. The Battle of Stirling Bridge was not just a military victory; it was also a declaration, a statement of Scottish resilience and courage. This victory sent shockwaves throughout England and established

Wallace as a symbol of Scottish defiance.

Following this triumph, Wallace was appointed as "Guardian of Scotland," a position that gave him considerable authority. Yet, the English were not easily deterred. A year after the stunning defeat at Stirling Bridge, on July 22nd, 1298, the stage was set for another epic clash: the Battle of Falkirk.

Wallace surveyed the battlefield with a sharp eye. He had chosen his ground carefully, positioning his seasoned warriors and raw recruits on a broad plain near Falkirk. The Scottish spearmen, who were arranged in close-knit formations called schiltrons, were like a thorny hedge against the English cavalry. However, unlike the Battle of Stirling Bridge, Wallace and his forces were up against a tougher opponent. They had to face the English army, led by King Edward I. It was made up of heavy cavalry and seasoned archers who were determined to put an end to the Scottish uprising.

The ground trembled beneath the thunderous charge of the English cavalry. The air was filled with the deadly whistling of arrows when the famed English longbowmen, a lethal addition to Edward's arsenal, unleashed their volleys. The Scottish schiltrons, though formidable against cavalry, were vulnerable to this rain of death.

Wallace was undaunted, though. He rallied his men, his voice cutting through the chaos. As a figure of hope amidst despair, he moved through the ranks, urging his men to hold their ground. For a time, the Scottish formations held firm, their pikes repelling the fierce charges of the English knights. However, the relentless barrage of arrows took its toll, as the deadly shafts accurately found their mark, piercing armor and flesh.

The battle soon turned into a maelstrom of violence and bloodshed. The English cavalry exploited the gaps opened by the archers and charged into the heart of the Scottish ranks. The schiltrons began to buckle and break under the unyielding pressure. Wallace fought bravely, his sword moving quickly as he tried to hold back the enemy, but the odds were stacked against him.

As the sun dipped low, casting long shadows over the field of Falkirk, the battle drew to its grim conclusion. The Scottish army was routed, their lines shattered, leaving the field littered with the bloodied bodies of the fallen. Wallace was forced to flee.

The Battle of Falkirk was a devastating blow to the Scottish cause, and it was a bitter lesson in the cruelty of war. Wallace's military career never fully recovered from this setback. Despite the loss, Wallace's spirit remained unbroken. He continued to fight for Scottish independence, though his tactics shifted more toward guerrilla warfare. However, his resistance came to an end in 1305 when he was betrayed and captured by the English.

Wallace's trial and execution in London were designed to be a spectacle of English power and a warning to other would-be rebels. After being convicted of high treason, he was subjected to the most horrific execution of the medieval era. He was dragged naked behind a horse to the location of his execution. He was then hung and emasculated while still breathing. His private parts were burned before his eyes. Only then did the executioner cut him open and quartered his lifeless body. The four parts were transported to Newcastle, Berwick, Perth, and Stirling to be publicly displayed.

A depiction of Wallace's trial in Westminster Hall.
https://commons.wikimedia.org/wiki/File:The_Trial_of_William_Wallace_at_Westminster.jpg

Wallace became an immortal symbol of Scotland's struggle for freedom. His name became synonymous with resistance against oppression, and his story was a rallying cry for those who valued liberty over life. The brutal manner of his death only further cemented his status as a martyr for Scottish independence.

Over the centuries, the legend of William Wallace grew, with his life and deeds taking on mythic proportions. He became not just a historical figure but also a symbol of national identity, embodying the resilience, courage, and undying spirit of the Scottish people. His story, immortalized in ballads, literature, and even in iconic films like *Braveheart*, continues to inspire and resonate with Scots and freedom-lovers around the world.

Robert the Bruce

While the sun set on the Battle of Falkirk, a new dawn was quietly rising in the form of another hero, Robert the Bruce. Born into the aristocracy on July 11th, 1274, his early life was filled with noble duties and court intrigues, which was a stark contrast to Wallace's humble upbringing. The young Robert grew up in a Scotland torn apart by the strife of the First War of Scottish Independence. This challenging environment shaped him, mixing his sense of loyalty and ambition with a strong desire for freedom.

Robert, with his sharp mind and charming personality, navigated through the treacherous waters of Scottish politics with a deft hand. Initially, he chose to show his allegiance to King Edward I of England, but this was nothing but a decision based on practicality. Deep down, Robert the Bruce was a true Scotsman who had an undying love for his homeland. This inner struggle defined much of his early life as he wrestled with his role in the ongoing struggle for Scotland's independence.

The turning point for Robert came with the death of Wallace. In 1306, in a bold move, Robert the Bruce claimed the Scottish crown. His coronation was a defiant proclamation of Scotland's enduring spirit. However, his path to the throne was not without peril. The English viewed his coronation as an act of treachery and intensified their efforts to subdue Scotland.

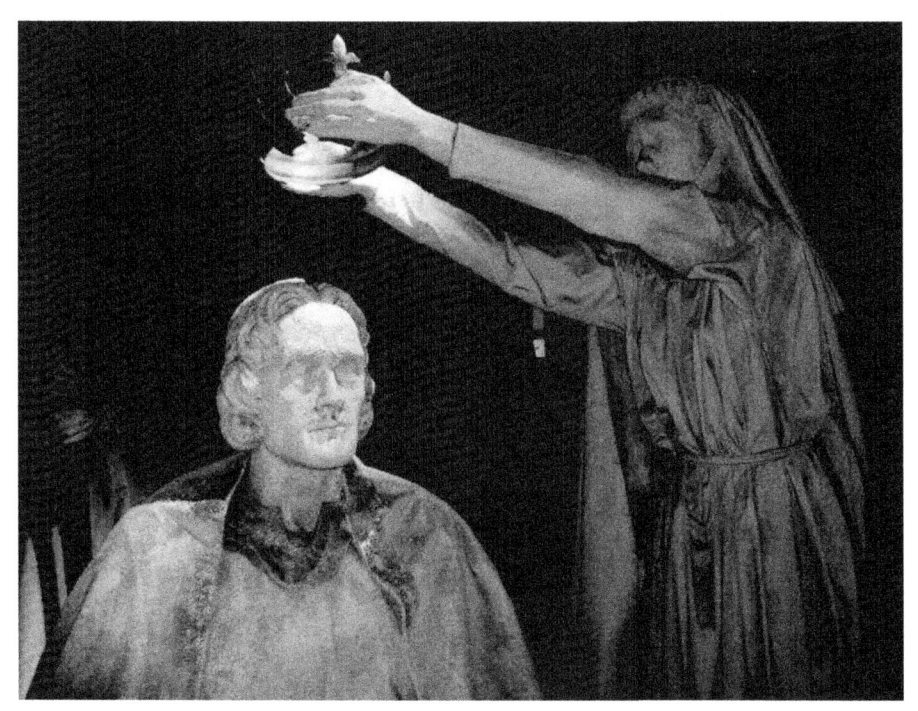

Robert the Bruce crowned as the king of the Scots.
Kim Traynor, CC BY-SA 3.0 <https://creativecommons.org/licenses/by-sa/3.0>, via Wikimedia Commons: https://commons.wikimedia.org/wiki/File:Robert_The_Bruce_Crowned_King_of_Scots.jpg

Robert's early reign was marked by a series of setbacks and defeats. He was forced into hiding. His forces were scattered, and his kingdom was in disarray. However, these tough times only made him more determined. From the shadows, he waged a guerrilla war against the English, using clever and unexpected strategies. Slowly, he regained strength, rallying the Scottish clans to his cause.

The culmination of Robert's struggle came in the summer of 1314 at the Battle of Bannockburn. The English, led by Edward II, sought to crush the Scottish rebellion once and for all. They marched north with a massive army, confident in their numbers and might. But Robert the Bruce, ever the strategist, picked the perfect spot for the battle. Near the Bannock Burn (a stream to the southwest of Stirling), he prepared his forces. These men had been toughened by years of unrest and fighting, and they were ready for the chance to fight once more for their freedom.

As the English approached, the vastly outnumbered Scottish army braced for the assault. Robert the Bruce, astride his horse, spoke to his men, calling them to arms. The battle commenced with the Scots employing tight schiltrons, their spears serving as a death sentence for the English cavalry. Robert led from the front. He was a whirlwind in battle, his prowess and leadership turning the tide.

The English became bogged down by the marshy ground and were taken aback by the intensity of the Scottish defense. They began to falter. Seeing their chance, the Scottish army launched a powerful counterattack, believing in their imminent victory. The English lines crumbled, turning their orderly retreat into a panicked flight. Bannockburn turned out to be a tremendous win for the Scots, showcasing Robert the Bruce's leadership skills and the indomitable spirit of his people.

The aftermath of Bannockburn was a turning point in the war. Scotland's independence was effectively secured, though skirmishes and political struggles would continue. Robert the Bruce's reign, post-Bannockburn, was marked by efforts to consolidate his kingdom and secure Scotland's future. He worked tirelessly to strengthen his realm, seeking diplomatic recognition and stability for his people.

In his later years, Robert the Bruce's health began to deteriorate. Yet, his determination and dedication to Scotland never declined. He passed away on June 7th, 1329, but his impact went far beyond his lifetime. Under his leadership, Scotland became a reborn nation.

Robert the Bruce, much like William Wallace before him, became a legend in Scotland. His life and actions became a key part of what it means to be a proud Scot today. His story continues to inspire new generations.

Black Agnes

Scotland also witnessed a woman with incredible determination and an unbreakable spirit come to the forefront. This female figure made such a strong impact that her name is now immortalized in Scottish history.

An illustration of Black Agnes from a children's storybook published in 1906.
https://commons.wikimedia.org/wiki/File:Black_Agnes,_from_a_children%27s_history_book.jpg

    Agnes Randolph, Countess of Dunbar and March, was nicknamed "Black Agnes" due to her distinctive dark hair and eyes. As the lady of Dunbar Castle, she was in charge of protecting the fortress, which was located in a crucial position near the southeastern coast of Scotland. Her moment of legend came in 1338 when William Montagu, the 1ˢᵗ Earl of Salisbury, and his formidable English army laid siege to Dunbar Castle. Montagu was undeniably an experienced leader, but his constant victories sometimes blurred his assumptions. Since the castle was under a woman's leadership, he thought it would be easy to capture. Little did he know that he would meet a foe as unyielding as the very stones of Dunbar itself.

    The siege began with a traditional display of might: a volley of rocks hurled by trebuchets. This tactic was designed to shatter both the walls and the people's resolve. But Agnes wasn't fazed by this attack. In a bold move, she had her maids wipe down the castle battlements with handkerchiefs, a gesture of contempt that angered Montagu and his soldiers.

As the days stretched into weeks, the English laid relentless assaults against the castle's defenses. Yet, under Agnes's command, the garrison fought back with a tenacity that belied their small numbers. In one of the siege's most dramatic moments, Montagu captured Agnes's brother, John Randolph, 3rd Earl of Moray, and threatened to execute him before the castle walls. Agnes retorted that his death would only make her the heir to their family's land. Eventually, her brother was spared. It was not done out of mercy but because the English realized their threat possessed no power over her iron will.

Throughout the siege, Agnes's leadership was a source of inspiration for her people. Her wit, courage, and relentless defiance were key to keeping the castle's defense strong. She rallied her troops, uplifted her subjects, and, according to legend, even taunted her enemies with insults, further inflaming their frustration.

What remains of Dunbar Castle today.
Kim Traynor, CC BY-SA 3.0 <https://creativecommons.org/licenses/by-sa/3.0>, via Wikimedia Commons: https://commons.wikimedia.org/wiki/File:Ruins_of_Dunbar_Castle,_East_Lothian_Scotland.jpg

After five long months, the siege of Dunbar Castle ended not with a bang but with a whimper. The weary and demoralized English gave up. They lifted the siege and retreated, their spirits crushed by the weight of

Agnes's otherworldly resistance. Agnes's name, "Black Agnes of Dunbar," echoed through Scottish history as a symbol of the strong resistance and undaunted courage of Scotland's daughters.

These legendary figures have become etched into the very soul of Scotland. They are not figments of imagination or relics of a bygone era. They are living, breathing presences in the Scottish consciousness.

Their stories carry a deep sense of meaning. They were shared over and over again, not only for fun around the fireplace but also to teach each new generation about their identity and to instill pride in them. Just as the Greek epics taught lessons of heroism and the Roman tales spoke of civic duty and empire, the Scottish legends served as a compass, guiding the Scots to stay true to their cultural and national values.

Chapter 3: Deities and Spirits: The Pantheon of Scottish Mythology

The stories of the Irish gods are particularly striking, each one equipped with colorful journeys. These stories were not just limited to the vast lands of Ireland; they spread far and wide, finding a special place in the hearts of the Scottish people as well. Among these gods, Lugh, known for his grandeur and strength, held an important role in both Irish and Scottish mythologies.

Our tale begins in an age when the world was young, and the lands of Ireland lay under the shadow of the Fomorians. This ancient race, believed to be from under the sea or the underworld, was as formidable as they were fearsome. Descriptions of them vary, with some accounts depicting them with the grotesque heads of goats and bodies created from the very elements of chaos. They were the embodiment of destructive natural forces. Scholars believe their appearance symbolizes the untamed and wild aspects of nature.

Depiction of the Fomorians.
https://commons.wikimedia.org/wiki/File:The_Fomorians,_Duncan_1912.jpg

At the helm of this race was Balor of the Baleful Eye, a king whose very gaze wrought destruction. When Balor's eye was opened, it could scorch the earth and lay waste to entire armies. Under his reign, the Fomorians brought unspeakable chaos upon the land, waging wars and enslaving peoples. Their most relentless adversaries were the Tuatha Dé Danann, a race of deities and skilled warriors. The ongoing conflict between the Fomorians and the Tuatha Dé Danann was fueled by land disagreements and deep-rooted hostilities.

The Tuatha Dé Danann as depicted in John Duncan's *The Riders of the Sidhe* (1911).
https://commons.wikimedia.org/wiki/File:Riders_of_th_Sidhe_(big).jpg

However, there was a prophecy that terrified Balor. This prophecy foretold his doom at the hands of his own grandson. To prevent this from coming true, Balor locked his daughter, Ethniu, in a tower of crystal, away from the world of men.

But destiny always has a way of fulfilling itself. Despite his efforts to change his fate, the world saw the birth of Lugh, who was predicted to take his grandfather's life. Lugh's hair looked like spun gold, and his eyes mirrored the ocean's depths. He was a stark contrast to Balor. He was a figure who inspired both awe and admiration. Lugh was known for his many talents. He was an artist, a powerful warrior, and a wise being. His heritage was a mix of the divine and mortal, combining the lineage of both the Fomorians and the Tuatha Dé Danann.

Lugh's journey eventually led him to the Hill of Tara, the seat of the Tuatha Dé Danann's king, Nuada. His attempt to join Nuada's court was initially met with resistance. The doorkeeper refused to let him in, claiming that the court already had experts in each skill Lugh claimed to have. Lugh then pointed out that no one had all his skills, which was what got him inside. Just as he expected, his versatility impressed Nuada, who saw in Lugh the potential to lead the Tuatha Dé Danann to victory against their oppressors.

Lugh's arrival at the court was a turning point. He triumphed over the king's champion and deity, Ogma, in a contest of strength and entertained the court with his harp playing. As time passed, Lugh noticed how the Tuatha Dé Danann were slowly accepting their fate. Not fond of the fact that the Fomorians held the higher ground, Lugh pledged to guide them to liberation. Nuada recognized Lugh's leadership and skill and appointed him as the commander of the Tuatha Dé Danann.

So, the stage was set for the legendary Battle of Mag Tuireadh. Lugh, who led the fight, was unstoppable, wielding his spear and sling with lethal accuracy. The battle was fierce, filled with clashing swords and magical powers. Unfortunately, King Nuada met his end during this intense fight. He was slain by the evil Balor.

The battle reached its peak in a fateful showdown. Lugh finally confronted his grandfather, Balor, in a duel that was about more than just physical strength; it was also a battle of fate and will. With cunning and skill, Lugh managed to turn Balor's destructive gaze upon himself by hitting his grandfather's eye with his sling. This act fulfilled the prophecy. Balor was defeated, and with his fall, the Fomorians' reign of terror ended.

The conclusion of the battle marked a new era for Ireland. The land began to thrive under the Tuatha Dé Danann's care. Lugh's victory freed the land from turmoil and disorder. The details of Lugh's final days remain shrouded in mystery. Some tales speak of a tragic demise at the hands of his own kin, a fate all too common among the gods. Others believe he simply faded from the world, his spirit becoming one with the very lands he fought to protect.

Lugh's influence lives on in the myths and legends of Ireland and Scotland. His story continues to enchant people, showing the lasting impact of myths and the timeless stories of ancient gods and heroes.

Bridie

Bridie, often likened to the Irish goddess Brigid, reigns as a deity of profound grace and nurturing power. Her essence, deeply rooted in the cycle of the seasons, manifests as the guardian of healing, childbirth, and the harbinger of spring. In Bridie's presence, the land awakens, and life blooms anew with the promise of renewal and growth.

Bridie's appearance, a blend of gentleness and formidable strength, mirrors the nurturing essence of the earth. Her hair, shining like the golden light of early morning, and her eyes, serene as tranquil waters, symbolize her deep connection to the rebirth of life. Dressed in robes that sparkle with the bright palettes of spring, Bridie was believed to walk through the green meadows and woods, leaving in her wake a trail of blossoming flora and revived life.

In both Scottish and Irish folktales, Bridie's tales resonate with the miracle of healing and the rejuvenation of the land after winter's cold embrace. Revered as the protector of livestock and the guardian of fertility, people often called on her in difficult times, hoping for her help to make their crops and animals thrive. Her festival, Imbolc, marks the beginning of spring. It's a time of celebration and renewal where her followers come together around holy fires to pay tribute to her ability to bring change and create new life.

One particular tale recounts Bridie's evolution from a pagan goddess to a revered Christian saint. This tale blends elements of myth, history, and spiritual change. It takes place during a time when Scotland's religious beliefs were evolving. In the story, Bridie's sacred flame, which was once lit in her honor in old forests, and her wells and springs, which were known for healing the sick, find a new place in Christian monasteries. Her monastery at Kildare, for one, became a center of learning and healing. There, her sacred flame burns continuously and is tended by her devoted nuns.

An illustration of Bridie or Brigid.
https://commons.wikimedia.org/wiki/File:Thecomingofbrideduncan1917.jpg

This story also delves into the miraculous feats associated with Saint Brigid, each echoing Bridie's ancient powers. From healing the sick to the miraculous multiplication of food, Saint Brigid's acts are a reflection of Bridie's divine qualities and influence. The narrative draws parallels between Bridie's role in heralding spring and Saint Brigid's celebration on February 1st, the day marking the beginning of spring in the Christian calendar. This story of transformation and endurance reflects the enduring nature of myths and the adaptability of divine figures through changing eras. Bridie, in her transition to Saint Brigid, became a bridge between the old and the new world.

Other tales highlight Saint Brigid's miraculous deeds, such as her cloak expanding to claim land for her monastery and her ability to turn water into beer to feed the poor. These miracles, while rooted in Christian lore, echo Bridie's ancient connection to the land and her power to nourish and protect.

Stained glass featuring Saint Brigid.
Octave 444, CC BY-SA 4.0 <https://creativecommons.org/licenses/by-sa/4.0>, via Wikimedia Commons: https://commons.wikimedia.org/wiki/File:Sainte_Brigitte_%C3%A9glise_Macon.jpg

Cernunnos

Cernunnos is known as a deity whose presence is strongly felt in the ancient Celtic lands, including the mystical realms of Scotland. This enigmatic figure, with the majesty of a god yet the mystery of the untamed wilds, is a mediator between man and nature. He was believed to be a silent guardian of the forests and their creatures.

The deity is often depicted with the antlers of a stag, which scholars suggest embodies the primal power and grace of nature. His appearance, a blend of human and beast, symbolizes his deep connection with all living things. He is often shown seated in a lordly pose, antlers rising proudly from his head. His wise and deep gaze seems to transcend time, holding within it the secrets of the ancient and mysterious woods.

The history of Cernunnos is shrouded in the mists of time, with only fragments of his story surviving. Researchers suggest he was a god of fertility, wealth, and the underworld, but a lot about him is still unclear. The Pillar of the Boatmen, an ancient artifact, gives us one of the few images of Cernunnos. Another striking depiction of this horned god is found on the Gundestrup Cauldron, believed to date back to 200 BCE. Here, he is shown in majestic splendor, adorned with torcs and surrounded by animals, perhaps highlighting his role as a master of beasts. He was seen as a ruler who could bring predator and prey together in harmony.

A depiction of an antlered deity, possibly Cernunnos, on the Gundestrup Cauldron. *Nationalmuseet, CC BY-SA 3.0 <https://creativecommons.org/licenses/by-sa/3.0>, via Wikimedia Commons: https://commons.wikimedia.org/wiki/File:Gundestrupkedlen-00054_(cropped).jpg*

Despite his compelling image, Cernunnos remains a figure of mystery. There are no myths or legends directly tied to his name. Some scholars believe Shakespeare's character Herne the Hunter might be based on Cernunnos. In Shakespeare's portrayal, Herne is a ghostly hunter who haunts Windsor Forest. The tale goes that Herne was a keeper of the forest favored by King Richard II, who admired his hunting skills. However, Herne's story takes a tragic turn when he gains the jealousy of the other hunters.

One day, while on a hunt, the king was attacked by a stag. Herne courageously intervened, saving the king, although he ended up mortally wounded himself. As he lay dying, a mysterious figure, often interpreted as a wizard or dark magician, appeared before him. He offered to save Herne's life on one condition: the famed hunter must give up his hunting skills. Desperate and not prepared to proceed to the afterlife, Herne agreed. And so, he miraculously recovered, but as promised, he lost his prowess in hunting.

Shunned and disgraced, Herne was driven to despair. In his anguish, he ventured into the forest. He attached his antlered helmet to a tree and took his own life. Because of this, legend says that Herne's spirit was doomed to haunt Windsor Forest. He was often depicted riding a horse and wearing antlers on his head. He was accompanied by the sounds of howling hounds and a wild hunt. His appearance was considered an omen of bad luck or misfortune.

However, the story of Herne the Hunter has evolved over the centuries. Some versions suggest that his spirit was actually a protector of the forest, though there are others that portray him as a malevolent entity. Theories about his origins range from him being an ancient pagan deity to a later invention by Shakespeare. The connection to Cernunnos is drawn from the shared imagery of antlers and mastery over animals, but it remains a topic of debate among scholars.

The possible link between Cernunnos and Saint Ciarán further blurs the line between pagan deities and Christian saints, suggesting a continuity and adaptation of ancient beliefs into the Christian era. This connection, while tenuous, speaks to the enduring presence of Cernunnos in the cultural and spiritual landscape of the Celts.

Despite the scant details and the lack of surviving stories, Cernunnos has not faded into obscurity. Instead, he has been reborn in the realms of pop culture and modern pagan practice. His powerful and mysterious image continues to captivate the imagination, a reminder of a time when gods walked in the deep forests and whispered in the winds.

Angus

Angus Og, known as Aonghas Òg in Scotland and Oengus in Ireland, was a deity famed for his remarkable allure and complexity. He exudes the vibrancy of youth and the allure of love, making him a central figure in many stories. With his golden hair that mirrored the sun's brilliance and eyes that reflected the depth of the deepest lochs, Angus Og was the embodiment of beauty and youthful vigor.

In Scottish folklore, Angus Og was celebrated as the handsome son of the mighty Cailleach, who reigned over the harsh and biting winter months. This deity of youth hid in the enchanted realm of Tír na nÓg, where time stood still and age was but a distant memory. Here, in this land of everlasting youth, Angus spent the winter waiting for a sign that heralded the coming of spring.

One such dream came to him in the heart of winter. He dreamed of Bridie, who appeared as a maiden so beautiful that her very existence signaled the renewal of the earth and the awakening of all life; some suggest that Bridie and the goddess Brigid were the same figure. However, this dream was marred by a cruel reality. Bridie was imprisoned by the Cailleach, who was envious of her brilliance and beauty. The divine winter hag was intent on delaying the arrival of spring and did so by giving Bridie endless, impossible tasks. Her goal was to weaken Bridie's luminous presence, which threatened to end her own cold and dark rule.

Driven by love and the desire to restore balance to the seasons, Angus Og borrowed three days of warmth from August. Mounted on his white steed, the god of youth journeyed forth, piercing through the cold of winter. It was a race against both time and the unyielding grip of the Cailleach. His quest, spanning the breadth of the land, eventually led him to the winter hag's underground palace just as the first hints of spring were beginning to stir the world from its winter slumber.

The meeting between the two beautiful beings in the depths of the Cailleach's underground realm was a moment of awakening and change. When Angus's and Bridie's eyes met, the earth responded. Flowers burst into bloom, the grass turned lush green, and the air itself seemed to sing with the promise of life. Bridie, previously dressed in shabby clothes, now glowed in white robes adorned with silver and embellished with the first blooms of spring and summer. Their union, marked by a grand wedding ceremony, symbolized the triumph of love over the desolation of winter.

Yet, this moment of joy was fleeting, as the Cailleach, enraged by the disruption of her reign, chased them with storms and tempests. Mounted on her dark steed, the Cailleach was a harbinger of winter's lingering fury. The land was immediately caught in a battle of seasons. However, time was not on the divine hag's side, as her power began to wane. As she retreated to the Well of Youth for rejuvenation, her strength greatly diminished, she succumbed to a deep slumber. In her absence, Angus and Bridie ascended as the King and Queen of Summer, heralding a time of warmth, growth, and bountiful joy.

Blue Men of the Minch

In a time long past, as the Scottish sun slowly sank below the horizon, a small ship called the *Sea Whisperer* set sail from the rugged coasts of the Outer Hebrides, right off the west coast of mainland Scotland. Its crew, toughened by the salt and spray of many voyages, were bound for faraway lands, their hearts filled with the promise of adventure and the allure of the unknown.

The captain of the ship, a robust man with sun-bleached hair, steered his vessel with a steady hand. His crew, a mix of old friends and young lads, was eager to prove its worth. They worked together harmoniously, their laughter and songs mingling with the sounds of the ocean and the ship's gentle creaking.

As they ventured farther into the deep waters, a hush fell over the *Sea Whisperer*. The seasoned sailors knew they were nearing the Minch, a stretch of water whispered about in taverns and harbors. This was believed to be the home of the Na Fir Ghorma or the Blue Men of the Minch. Legends spoke of these creatures, saying they were beings who looked much like men save for their blue skin.

The Blue Men, it was said, were masters of the sea, capable of conjuring storms with a flick of their hand. In calm weather, they would drift, half-submerged and in a slumber as peaceful as the still sea. These creatures swam with their torsos above the water, moving with the elegance of friendly dolphins. Their eyes were said to gleam with the knowledge of age-old ocean tides and the secret of the sea's depths.

The captain, with both of his weathered hands firmly wrapped around the helm, kept a watchful eye for any peculiar signs coming from the ocean. According to legends and tales, if the Blue Men approached, their chief would present a challenge—a duel of wit and poetry. Failing to respond to their riddles could lead to catastrophe and unleash the fury of the deep sea itself.

As twilight deepened, an eerie stillness settled upon the waters. The crew grew silent as they felt the sudden change in the atmosphere. And then, as if conjured by their own thoughts, the Blue Men appeared. Their blue skin shimmered under the fading light, and their keen eyes, sharp as the horizon line, focused on the *Sea Whisperer*.

The chief of the Blue Men soon emerged, displaying his imposing figure to the wary sailors. His deep and resonant voice echoed across the waves, bouncing off the ship's hull. He shouted the first two lines of a cryptic verse, issuing his challenge directly to the captain:

"In the depths where shadows play,

Where the light of day fades away..."

The crew held their breath, their eyes locked on their captain, who stood firm at the helm. His mind raced, the lines of the verse turning in his head. He was well aware that the fate of the *Sea Whisperer* and her crew hung in the balance. Then, with a voice as steady as the North Star, the determined captain shouted back the completing lines of the verse:

"...We guard the secrets old and deep,

In the ocean's heart, where dreams do sleep."

It was as if the sea was holding its breath in anticipation. Then, the chief of the Blue Men burst into laughter, a sound almost resembling the rolling of distant thunder. This laughter was not to mock; instead, it was a sign of respect, a recognition of the captain's wit and worth. With just a simple nod, the Blue Men dove beneath the waves, plunging back into the depths, vanishing as swiftly as they had come.

The crew of the *Sea Whisperer* breathed a sigh of relief, thankful for their captain's quick thinking and for sparing them from the unpredictable wrath of the sea. The captain, with a grin as wide as the horizon, turned to his crew, his eyes sparkling with the thrill of the encounter.

"Tonight, we drink to the Blue Men," he announced. "To their riddles and the secrets of the ocean!"

The tale of their encounter with the Na Fir Ghorma became a legend, a story told in hushed tones around warm fires and over clinking beer mugs. This tale of the sea and its ancient inhabitants reminded everyone of the respect due to the ocean's mysteries.

Chapter 4: The Fae and the Underworld: Different Realms

We are never alone in the world. The universe is full of mystery, and nowhere is this more evident than in the heart of Scotland. According to old beliefs, here, among the blooming thistles and mist-covered hills, existed a world parallel to ours—a realm steeped in magic and mystery. This was the world of the Fae.

The Fae, or fairies, are not just figments of imagination; they are integral to Scottish mythology. They embody the essence of the land, the whisper of the wind through the heather, and the rustle of leaves in the ancient forests. The Fae exist in a realm that overlaps with our world but remains just out of sight, with some claiming it was accessible through ancient hills, hidden paths, or within the heart of wild places.

Some of the most well known of these beings are the inhabitants of the Seelie and Unseelie Courts. The Seelie Court, sometimes known as the "Blessed Ones," is often depicted as a procession of brilliant light gliding through the night air. These fairies love music and dancing, and they are known for their magnificent parties and celebrations under the serene, moonlit sky. These fairies are most active during nighttime, and more than often, their journeys are not just for fun; they often help those in need. The Seelie are very fond of humans, and while they are prone to mischief, especially when boredom strikes, their pranks are usually harmless, a reflection of their generally benevolent nature toward mankind.

The Code of the Seelie Court is a set of principles that govern the behavior of its members. This code emphasizes the following:

1. **Honor Above All:** For the Seelie, their honor is their most treasured possession. It is even more important than life. A Seelie would rather face death than endure the shame of dishonor, and they strive to never bring disgrace upon their kin.
2. **Love Conquers All:** The Seelie hold love in the highest regard, seeing it as the purest expression of the soul. While romantic love is esteemed the most, they also value strong friendships and non-romantic relationships.
3. **Beauty Is Life:** For the Seelie, beauty is paramount. They are naturally attracted to all forms of beauty and are willing to fight to preserve it, whether it's a person, a place, or an object.
4. **Never Forget a Debt:** The Seelie take debts seriously. They are committed to repaying them, whether they are favors or slights. They believe in repaying kindness promptly and seeking justice quickly for any wrongs done to them.

The Unseelie Court, on the other hand, is a darker assembly. Known as the "Unblessed Ones," they present a stark contrast to their Seelie counterparts. They are often envisioned as a dark cloud sweeping across the sky, their unnerving laughter and howls carrying on the wind. The Unseelie Fae are often described as less human in appearance, with wild, untamed features that reflect their more nefarious nature. Some are said to have glowing red eyes, sharp teeth, and claws, a stark contrast to the luminescent beauty of the Seelie Court.

While some suggest the Unseelie are not inherently evil, it is safe to assume that they are far from kind. They lean toward malevolence and often seek to harm or deceive humans. According to Scottish myths, they are sometimes portrayed as fallen Seelie who failed to meet the Seelie Court's strict standards of chivalry. As a result, the Unseelie Court became a haven for these outcasts, as well as for enslaved mortals and various monstrous creatures.

The Code of the Unseelie Court reflects their darker nature and consists of the following:

1. **Embracing Change:** The Unseelie embraces chaos, viewing stability as an illusion. They believe in adapting and evolving to thrive in a world that is always changing.

2. **Glamor is Free:** Glamor is a natural magic of the Daoine Sidhe or the Fae. It can be used to create illusions or cast enchantments. This natural magic is a favorite tool of the Unseelie. Unlike the more cautious Seelie, the Unseelie use this power without any hesitation, believing that any power not utilized is essentially wasted.
3. **Honor Is a Lie:** The Unseelie dismisses the idea of honor, focusing on self-interest instead. They find truth in self-pursuit rather than in meeting obligations to others.
4. **Prioritizing Passion:** For the Unseelie, living passionately is the most authentic way of life. They act on their instincts and desires, often ignoring duties or the repercussions of their actions.

The abilities of these fairies are as varied as their appearances. Some have the power to shape-shift, taking on forms of animals or even humans. Others wield magic that can either bless or curse and heal or harm. The Fae are also known for their skill in illusion. They are able to create glamors that can make the old appear young, the mundane seem magnificent, or even make themselves invisible to human eyes.

In Scottish folklore, encounters with the Fae are often cautionary tales. One such story tells of a young man who, on his way home, heard the enchanting music of a fairy celebration. Drawn by the melody, he found himself in the presence of the Seelie Court. He joined their dance, and when he finally left, he discovered that what felt like hours was actually years. Everyone he knew had aged or passed away. This tale serves as a reminder of the enchanting yet perilous nature of the fairy world.

Another tale speaks of the Unseelie Court's mischief. It tells of a farmer who encountered a group of these malevolent fairies one night. They demanded his help in their mischievous deeds, and fearing their wrath, he complied. The farmer spent the night aiding the Unseelie Fae in their pranks, only to find himself cursed at dawn, unable to speak of what he saw under penalty of death. This story illustrates the darker side of the Fae and their love for chaos and trickery.

The Scots also believed in the concept of the underworld, better known as the Otherworld in their vibrant folklore. However, since the Otherworld is shrouded in mist and mystery, it stands in stark contrast to the more defined afterlives of Greek and Egyptian mythology.

In the Greek underworld, ruled by Hades, the dead embark on a final journey across the River Styx, entering a shadowy realm separated from the living. This world beneath the earth is said to be a place of souls, a realm where justice reigns in the form of rewards or punishments. Egyptian mythology also portrays an intricate afterlife, where the dead traverse through trials and judgments under the watchful eyes of Osiris, the god of the dead, in a land beyond the living.

The Scottish Otherworld is not a singular realm of the dead. It is an ethereal, parallel dimension that coexists with our world, a place where the lines between the natural and the supernatural blur. This realm is not solely for the departed; it is a mysterious domain of the Fae, a land steeped in magic and home to beings both wondrous and fearsome.

Unlike the Greek and Egyptian conceptions, the Scottish Otherworld is closely intertwined with the fairy realm. It is a place that is ever-present, hidden behind ancient hills or veiled in the mists that often blanket the Scottish landscape. It is a world where time may flow differently, where the laws of nature are mere suggestions and often ignored by the mystical beings who live there.

In Scottish folklore, certain omens or signs are not necessarily indicators of someone's impending death; instead, they may be a gateway to a more mysterious world. These omens, deeply rooted in folklore, serve as both caution and temptation, leading some to their doom and others into the depths of the unknown. Typically, strange or even terrifying creatures and spirits carry the omens and display them to mortals.

The Tale of the Bean Nighe

In a small hamlet nestled in the shadow of the Scottish Highlands lived a humble peasant named Aoidh. With calloused hands and a gentle heart, Aoidh spent his days tending to his modest farm, living a simple yet content life. However, Aoidh's peaceful existence was about to be touched by the uncanny realm of Scottish myth.

One chilly autumn evening, as the sun dipped below the rugged hills, painting the sky in shades of crimson and gold, Aoidh decided to take a shortcut home through the woods. The forest, a maze of ancient trees and whispering leaves, had always been a place of solace for him. However, that night, it held an air of mystery that made him feel the soft brushes of terror and discomfort.

As he walked, accompanied only by sounds of the crunch of leaves under his foot, Aoidh's eyes were drawn to a figure by the stream, a strange solitary woman hunched over the water. Her presence was both unexpected and unsettling at the same time. Drawing closer, Aoidh saw that she was washing clothes, her hands working tirelessly in the cold, flowing water. But it was no ordinary laundry she washed; the clothes were stained with blood, the water turning a ghostly crimson-red with each scrub.

The sight rooted Aoidh to the spot, his heart pounding with fear and a pinch of fascination. He realized, with a shiver running down his spine, that he was in the presence of the Bean Nighe, the Washing Woman of Scottish lore. It was said that the Bean Nighe was a harbinger of death, washing the blood-stained clothes of those soon to meet their end.

Torn between terror and curiosity, Aoidh found his voice.

"Why do you wash these clothes in such a place and at such an hour?" he asked, his voice barely above a whisper.

The Bean Nighe paused, her hands stilling in the water. She raised her head, and Aoidh saw her face, sorrowful yet serene, as if carrying the weight of untold secrets.

"I wash the clothes of those whose time is near," she replied, her voice almost like the rustle of leaves. "I am the omen of what is to come, the link between this world and the Otherworld."

"Am I...am I to die?" he stuttered, a tremor in his voice.

The Bean Nighe looked at him, her eyes reflecting a depth of wisdom and sorrow.

"Not you, Aoidh, but someone close to your heart. I am sorry," she said, her voice tinged with a timeless sadness.

Aoidh felt a chill that had nothing to do with the serene autumn air. He thought of his family and friends. Who among them was marked by fate? The Bean Nighe returned to her washing, the sound of the water resembling a mournful melody in the growing darkness.

As he made his way home, the encounter replayed in his mind. He knew now that the Bean Nighe was more than a myth; she was a reminder of the thin veil between life and death, a messenger from the incomprehensible Otherworld, a place of mystery and enchantment that lay just beyond the reach of the living.

In the days that followed, Aoidh's life was touched by sorrow, as the omen of the Bean Nighe came to reality. He heard news that a young woman from a nearby village had suddenly died from an unknown disease. This woman was Aoidh's first love, the one he kept close to his heart for years despite their paths having diverged long ago. Her loss left a void in Aoidh's heart.

The Tale of the Cú-Sith, the Wolf That Brings Death

In another humble village nestled among the misty rolling hills and ancient woods, an old man sat by a crackling fire, surrounded by eager, youthful faces. Among them were two young boys known for their playful mischief and boundless curiosity. The old man began to tell a tale that had been passed down through generations—the tale of the Cú-Sith and Cat Sith, mysterious creatures of Scottish folklore.

"The Cú-Sith," he began, his voice low, "is a beast of legend, a fairy dog as large as a young cow, with fur as green as the mossy hillsides. It roams the highlands and the deep valleys, its presence heralded by three blood-curdling howls." The boys leaned in closer, their eyes wide. "Those who hear these howls must find shelter before the third, for it is said that those who do not will meet a terrifying fate."

He then spoke of the Cat Sith, a large black cat with a distinctive white spot on its chest. "The Cat Sith moves like a shadow in the night, silent and watchful. Some believe it to be a transformed witch or a fairy creature, a being that steals the souls of the dead before they can journey to the next world."

One of the boys hung onto every word with a mix of fear and awe. The other boy scoffed at the story. "Just old tales to scare children," he said, a smirk on his face.

As dusk fell that day, after hours of playing in the woods, the boys started their walk home. The sky was a canvas of darkening blues and purples, and the moon hung like a silver beacon. While walking, the believing boy saw, at the corner of his eyes, a cat-like figure slowly moving through the bushes. He thought of the Cat Sith. So, he stopped and looked around, perhaps hoping he could see the cat more clearly. But the creature was nowhere to be seen; it was as if it had disappeared into thin air. Assuming it was just another cat, the boy continued walking and eventually caught up with his friend, who was already several steps ahead.

Suddenly, the stillness of the night was shattered by an eerie and otherworldly howl. The believing boy's heart skipped a beat, especially after remembering the peculiar sighting of the cat earlier. His friend, who noticed the believing boy's face turning pale, burst into laughter.

"It's just a wolf," he said, emboldened by his disbelief. "Don't tell me you believe in the story?"

Driven by a mix of curiosity and bravado, the skeptical boy ventured deeper into the woods, determined to prove the howl was nothing more than a wild animal. His friend, gripped by the stories of old, refused to follow, his steps hastening toward the safety of the village.

As the fearful boy neared the village, a second howl echoed through the woods, more chilling than the first. He saw villagers rushing to their homes, their faces etched with concern. Without hesitation, he darted home just as the third howl, a sound that seemed to carry the weight of doom, filled the air.

The boy, now safe within his home, stared out into the darkness, thoughts of his friend lingering in his mind. The night passed, and morning light broke, but the brave boy did not return. Search parties combed the woods. Their calls were answered only by their own echoes. The boy was nowhere to be found. It was as if he had vanished, as if he had been claimed by the very legends he had mocked.

The village was abuzz with whispers of the Cú-Sith and the boy's bravery, along with the old man's story that had become a grim reality. The story of the two boys and their encounter with the unseen forces of Scottish lore became a stark reminder to all. Respect the legends and the old tales, for in the shadows of the Scottish highlands, the boundary between myth and reality is as fine as a strand of mist, and mythical beings are never too far away.

The old man would often retell the story. Each time, they seemed to gain a deeper understanding.

"Respect the legends," he would say, his voice resonating with the age-old wisdom of the land. "Our stories are more than just tales; they are echoes from an unseen world, a world much closer than you might think."

The Will-o'-the-Wisp

One late autumn evening, a daring young lad named Callum decided to explore the dense woods that bordered the village. He had grown up on tales of the will-o'-the-wisp, the flickering spirit light said to appear in the most desolate parts of the forest. The spirit was said to be responsible for the deaths of many villagers in the hilly regions of Scotland; almost everyone was told of the danger of following the will-o'-the-wisp. The spirit could not only lead unwary travelers into dense forests, full of mysteries and other unknown creatures, but it could also trick them into venturing perilously close to treacherous cliffs hidden within the dense foliage.

The will-o'-the-wisp and a snake.
https://commons.wikimedia.org/wiki/File:Will-o-the-wisp_and_snake_by_Hermann_Hendrich_1823.jpg

The will-o'-the-wisp, known for its mysterious and deceptive glow, had a knack for leading the curious and the foolhardy to the edges of steep cliffs. Shrouded by darkness and the dense underbrush, these cliffs were invisible until it was too late. Many a tale recounted in the village spoke of wanderers, entranced by the spirit's glow, stepping off into the abyss, their last moments marked by a chilling realization of the deceitful light.

However, Callum was an avid explorer with decades of experience under his belt. He was well versed in the language of the wilderness and skilled in reading the subtle signs of nature, from the direction of the wind to the patterns of the stars. In his heart, Callum believed that only fools could fall prey to the tricks of the will-o'-the-wisp. As an expert woodsman, he was confident in his ability to navigate any terrain, no matter how treacherous or unfamiliar.

With this unshakable confidence, Callum's curiosity about the will-o'-the-wisp grew ever stronger. He thought of it not as a threat but as a challenge, a test of his skills and experience. He was sure that he could outwit the spirit and uncover the secrets it guarded in the deep wilderness. To him, the tales of the will-o'-the-wisp leading people to their doom were nothing but stories for the gullible and the unskilled.

One moonlit night, Callum set out into the forest, determined to track down the elusive spirit. He moved with ease, his steps silent and sure, his eyes keenly observing every detail around him. As he ventured deeper, the familiar sights and sounds of the forest comforted him, reinforcing his belief in his mastery over the wild.

Callum's determination eventually bore fruit. He spotted the mysterious light of the will-o'-the-wisp twinkling between the trees. It moved with an elegant grace, always just out of reach yet never completely vanishing. Excited, Callum followed the light. He moved carefully but confidently, certain of his ability to retrace his steps.

The light led him on a winding path through the forest. He crossed over babbling streams and pushed through dense thickets. Callum's senses were heightened, keenly picking up any subtle changes around him. He noted landmarks, mentally mapping his route.

But as the night wore on, the forest seemed to transform. The trees appeared less familiar, the sounds more eerie, and the air grew thick with a mist that obscured the moon. Callum realized, with a rising sense of unease, that the landscape had changed subtly, almost imperceptibly, disorienting even his experienced eyes.

The light of the will-o'-the-wisp, which had initially drawn Callum in with its mystery, now appeared to taunt him with its elusive movements. Callum pushed on, refusing to admit that he might have underestimated the spirit. Suddenly, he found himself on the edge of a steep ravine, hidden by the dense fog and the deceptive light. It was at this moment that Callum realized the true nature of the will-o'-the-wisp. It was not just a physical guide leading travelers astray; it was also a master of illusion, capable of altering perceptions and challenging even the most experienced woodsman.

With a newfound respect for the legend and its dangers, Callum carefully retraced his steps, using all his skills to navigate back to familiar ground. He emerged from the forest as dawn broke, humbled and wiser. His encounter with the will-o'-the-wisp had taught him that even the most skilled are not immune to the powers of the Otherworld.

Back in the village, Callum shared his tale, not as a story of triumph but as a lesson in humility and respect for the ancient mysteries of the land. The will-o'-the-wisp remained a legend, a symbol of the wild, untamed spirit of the Scottish wilderness, and a reminder that some mysteries are best left unchallenged.

Chapter 5: Ghosts and Apparitions

Edinburgh, nestled in the heart of Scotland, is a city where the modern world intertwines with the past. Today, it bursts with a mix of contemporary culture and historical magnificence, but beneath its modern facade lies a deep and sometimes dark history.

In medieval Scotland, Edinburgh was more than just a city; it was the heart of a nation. The castles, including the renowned Edinburgh Castle, were not just residences but also symbols of power and protection. Built on a rock, the castle overlooked the city, a guardian against invaders and a stronghold for the rulers of Scotland. These castles were the epicenters of political power and military might. They were designed to withstand sieges and protect their inhabitants from the tumultuous world outside.

Edinburgh Castle.
Kim Traynor, CC BY-SA 3.0 <https://creativecommons.org/licenses/by-sa/3.0>, via Wikimedia Commons: https://commons.wikimedia.org/wiki/File:Edinburgh_Castle_from_the_North.JPG

Yet, amidst the tangible history of battles and kings, a different kind of legacy lingers in Edinburgh's cobbled streets and ancient buildings—a legacy of secrets, myths, and eerie tales.

Among these secrets was a network of hidden tunnels beneath Edinburgh Castle. They were believed to have been constructed for covert purposes, perhaps as secret escape routes for royalty or as a means to move unseen during times of war or political turmoil. While their true purpose remains shrouded in mystery, the rediscovery of these secret tunnels eventually led to the beginning of a haunting story popularly known as the Ghost Piper of Edinburgh Castle.

The legend goes that immediately after the discovery of the tunnels, the city's leaders announced that they needed someone to explore the labyrinthine network. They wanted to unravel the mystery of these subterranean passageways. Thus, for unknown reasons, a young piper was chosen to carry out this task. In the boy's eyes, his mission was simple: he was to navigate the network of tunnels while playing his pipes so that those above could trace his progress through the melodies echoing from below.

The young piper delved into the darkness. The tune coming from his bagpipes resonated through the streets, creating an otherworldly atmosphere that captivated the city. People paused in their daily chores, listening intently as the haunting notes floated up from the depths. Some followed the sound, tracking his path through the city, while others were tasked with creating a map of the tunnels based on the rough location of the boy deep underneath the cobblestone streets.

But then, something chilling occurred. In the midst of his exploration, the music stopped abruptly. The silence that followed was deafening, a stark contrast to the lively tunes that had filled the air moments before. The last notes were heard near Tron Kirk. Reports were presumably made to the city's leaders. Almost immediately, a frantic search was mounted, but no trace of the young piper was ever found. He had vanished, mysteriously swallowed by the labyrinth beneath the city. In the wake of his mysterious disappearance, the tunnels were sealed as if to bury the secret of what happened to the young piper. However, the story does not end there.

Today, it is said that the eerie sound of bagpipes can still be heard beneath the streets of Edinburgh, especially near the castle. The music is a haunting reminder of the boy who never returned, his spirit seemingly trapped in the labyrinth, playing his pipes in a perpetual search for a way out. Perhaps he is waiting for someone to rescue him from his eternal entrapment.

These ghostly melodies are not constant. They occur at unexpected moments, sending shivers down the spines of those who hear them. The whispers of the past seem louder in the quiet of the night. Some say it is nothing but the wind, while others believe it is the young piper's ghost, still wandering the tunnels, lost and alone.

The Ghost Piper of Edinburgh Castle is just one of many ghostly tales from Scotland's past. Another haunting narrative resides in the shadowy halls of Crathes Castle.

Built in the 16th century by Alexander Burnett, the castle rose from the Royal Forest of Drum. This classic Scottish tower-house-style castle, with its imposing structure, began its construction in 1553. However, its completion was delayed, largely due to the political unrest involving Mary, Queen of Scots. The castle was finally finished in 1596.

The story of Crathes Castle is intertwined with the dark and tragic tale of the Burnetts of Leys. Before the castle's construction, the Burnetts resided in a house near a loch, a place that became the scene of a chilling event. This event, marked by death and spectral hauntings, would forever alter the destiny of the Burnett family.

It began with Alexander Burnett, a young lord who came under the strict supervision of his controlling mother, Lady Agnes, following his father's passing. Alexander's life took a fateful turn when he fell in love with Bertha, a distant cousin who had been entrusted to his family's care. However, their blossoming love was to be short-lived. Alexander, having been away, returned to find Bertha on her deathbed.

In a moment of profound grief, Alexander reached for a goblet of wine, perhaps to share a final drink with his beloved, but Lady Agnes intervened. With a swift motion, she snatched the goblet from his hand and hurled it out the window. It was then that a horrifying truth dawned on Alexander: his mother had poisoned Bertha. Lady Agnes had always displayed her disapproval whenever Alexander expressed his fondness for Bertha. She was said to have another plan for his son; she wished for him to marry into a noble family instead.

The tragedy at the Loch house took a more sinister turn months later. Bertha's father arrived, intending to bring his daughter home, only to be confronted with the grim news of her death. As Lady Agnes attempted to explain the circumstances, a bone-chilling cold swept through the room. Suddenly, Lady Agnes, her eyes wide with terror, screamed, "She comes! She comes!" and suddenly fell dead to the floor, frozen.

Plagued by the haunting events and the specter of death, the Burnetts abandoned their old Loch house and sought refuge in Crathes Castle, hoping to leave behind the ghosts of their past. However, the spirits would not be so easily forgotten. On the anniversary of Bertha's death, a phantom spirit known as the White Lady is said to make the journey from the old Loch house to Crathes Castle. Some believe this ghostly figure to be Bertha, stuck forever seeking justice and peace. Others whisper that it is none other than Lady Agnes, cursed to relive her treachery for eternity.

Crathes Castle.
Oyoyoy, CC BY-SA 3.0 <https://creativecommons.org/licenses/by-sa/3.0>, via Wikimedia Commons: https://commons.wikimedia.org/wiki/File:Crathes_Castle_from_garden.jpg

Crathes Castle is home to multiple ghost stories. There's also the haunting account of the Green Lady.

The Green Lady is often spotted silently gliding through the rooms and hallways of Crathes Castle. She is believed to be a former inhabitant of the castle, but her identity has been lost to the ages. She is most often seen in a specific room, now named the Green Lady's Room. Her appearances are always accompanied by a sudden drop in temperature and a subtle scent of rosemary, a herb traditionally associated with remembrance.

Legend has it that the Green Lady was a servant girl at Crathes Castle who fell victim to a tragic fate. The most common telling of her story suggests a tale of forbidden love and heartbreak. She was believed to have fallen in love with a nobleman residing at the castle, a love that was doomed from the start due to their different social standings. Their secret romance ended in tragedy when the girl found herself with child.

Faced with the harsh realities of her situation and the unforgiving societal norms of the time, the Green Lady's fate took a dark turn. It is said that she vanished mysteriously, with whispers suggesting that she might have been killed to prevent a scandal or perhaps took her own life.

Many years after the Green Lady's mysterious vanishing, something unsettling was found during renovations at the castle. Workers uncovered the skeletal remains of a woman and a child concealed behind a fireplace in the Green Lady's Room. This grim find gave a hauntingly real aspect to the ghost stories, hinting that the Green Lady's unsettled spirit could be roaming the castle, grieving her lost love and the child she never had the chance to raise.

To this day, the Green Lady's spirit lingers in the Crathes Castle. Visitors and staff members often report seeing her spectral form. Some even say they feel a deep sense of sorrow in the room where she was last seen, the room now named after her. Others describe an eerie sensation of being watched or catching glimpses of a figure in green out of the corner of their eye, only for it to vanish as soon as they turn to look directly at it. A few also claim that they heard distant voices warning them not to enter the room, causing them to hesitate and turn back.

Hermitage Castle

Hermitage Castle, nestled in the rugged borderlands of Scotland, holds stories of intrigue, betrayal, and ghostly whispers within its imposing walls. This formidable fortress, often referred to as "the guardhouse of the bloodiest valley in Britain," has stood since the 12th century.

Hermitage Castle in 1814.
https://commons.wikimedia.org/wiki/File:Hermitagecastle1814.jpg

One of the most notable episodes in the castle's history involves Sir William Douglas, known as "the Knight of Liddesdale." In 1338, during the Wars of Scottish Independence, Douglas wrestled Hermitage Castle from the clutches of its English occupant, Sir Ralph Neville. The seizure of Hermitage was a strategic victory, with Douglas employing a combination of military prowess and cunning tactics. His success in these conflicts earned him a formidable reputation and significant respect in Scotland, marking him as a key figure in the struggle against English domination.

However, Sir William's story becomes more complex and darker with the appearance of Sir Alexander Ramsay. Ramsay, another distinguished Scottish knight, rose to prominence and was appointed as the sheriff of Teviotdale, a position that Douglas long had his eyes on. Ramsay's growing influence and success, particularly his capture of

Roxburgh Castle from the English, only fueled Douglas's envy and resentment.

Driven by jealousy, Sir William Douglas conceived a sinister plan. He lured Sir Alexander Ramsay to Hermitage Castle under the guise of friendship or for a meeting. However, upon Ramsay's arrival, Douglas's true intentions were revealed. Ramsay was seized and thrown into a deep, dark dungeon within the castle's bowels. This "frightful pit," as it came to be known, was a place of unimaginable horrors. Devoid of light, air, and even basic sanitation, it was more like a living tomb. It was far worse than the cells that held the most notorious criminals or the dens that housed the world's wildest animals.

In this ghastly dungeon, Sir Alexander Ramsay suffered a fate worse than death. He was left to starve with no hope of rescue. The conditions were so dire that it was said he resorted to eating pieces of his own flesh before he finally succumbed to death's embrace. Ramsay's tragic demise was more than just a tale of brutal revenge; it's a stark illustration of the unforgiving and relentless quest for power among medieval Scottish nobility.

The ghostly legacy of this dark deed has haunted Hermitage Castle ever since. It is said that the anguished groans of Sir Alexander Ramsay echo through the castle. Visitors to Hermitage have reported hearing unsettling sounds emanating from the depths of the castle, almost as if the very stones themselves are reliving the horrors of the past.

However, not all ghostly tales surrounding Hermitage Castle are terrifying and eerie. Among the castle's storied past is a tale of love and dedication involving one of Scotland's most famous historical figures, Mary, Queen of Scots.

The story takes us back to the 16th century, during the tumultuous period of Mary's reign. One of the central figures in her life was James Hepburn, 4th Earl of Bothwell, a man who would eventually become Mary's third husband. Bothwell, a loyal supporter of Mary, was often involved in the political and military unrest of the time.

On one fateful occasion, Lord Bothwell found himself gravely wounded following a skirmish with border reivers, who were an infamous band of raiders in the area between Scotland and England. The news of his injury reached Mary, Queen of Scots, who was staying in Jedburgh at the time, approximately fifty miles away from Hermitage Castle, where Bothwell was recovering.

Upon hearing of Bothwell's condition, Mary made a daring decision. She resolved to visit Bothwell. It was a journey fraught with danger, not only because of the distance but also due to the chaotic political climate and the rough terrain she would have to traverse. Undeterred, Mary set out on her journey, riding through the rugged landscape of the Scottish Borders. Her ride to Hermitage Castle became legendary for its speed and her determination. Mary covered the fifty-mile distance in just a single day, an impressive achievement given the travel difficulties of the period.

Upon her arrival at Hermitage Castle, Mary found Bothwell in a dire state, though, fortunately, he survived. Mary's return journey proved to be even more harrowing. The journey, coupled with the stress and strain of the situation, took a significant toll on her health.

Upon her return to Jedburgh, Mary fell gravely ill. She developed a fever so severe that it nearly claimed her life. Her visit to Hermitage, though brief, was a poignant moment, reflecting the depth of her concern for her future husband. This act of bravery and devotion adds a bright light to the otherwise grim history of Hermitage Castle. Today, some claim they caught a glimpse of the apparitions of Mary and Bothwell walking around the castle, their hands tightly wrapped around each other.

Mary King's Close

In the center of Edinburgh, along the famous Royal Mile, stands the Edinburgh City Chambers, a prominent and stately building. This impressive structure holds a secret buried beneath its foundations: a hidden network of streets and homes known as Mary's Close.

This close, which was built in the 17th century, was named after Mary King, a well-known merchant of the time. Her name became forever linked to this hidden corner of the city, marking a place that once buzzed with life but now echoes with the tales of its haunting past.

Mary King's Close, Edinburgh.
https://commons.wikimedia.org/wiki/File:Marykingsclose006.jpg

Imagine seeing this close through the eyes of a young man named John, who lived there in the 17th century. For him and his neighbors, life in Mary's Close was a daily struggle. The streets were narrow and dark, with houses piled upon each other (sometimes rising up to seven stories). Those with more wealth were said to have lived on the top floors, while the less unfortunate ones inhabited the lower stories. To put it simply, Mary's Close was a cramped labyrinth of shadowy passageways. While the place was teeming with life, the air was also filled with the filth and stench of an era devoid of modern sanitation.

In John's time, Mary's Close was marred by the absence of a proper sewage system. Residents, John included, had to deal with the daily challenge of getting rid of their own waste. Each household was equipped with a bucket, which was their only means of managing waste. When the bucket was full, they would wait for a shout of "Gardy Loo!" from the streets. This shout marked that it was time to throw the waste out onto the street. The waste would flow down the streets in little channels, eventually ending up in a big, dirty manmade lake called Nor' Loch, where the Princes Street Gardens are now.

This lack of sanitation definitely made Mary's Close a breeding ground for disease, and it was also here that the Black Death found fertile ground in 1645. The plague tore through the cramped quarters with ruthless efficiency, leaving nothing but a trail of death and despair. In a desperate, misguided attempt to halt the spread of the contagion, the city's authorities made a harrowing decision. They sealed off the neighborhood, trapping the residents within the plague-ridden close.

John, along with his neighbors, faced a grim fate as the walls went up. Left to die in conditions of unimaginable horror, Mary's Close became a tomb for its inhabitants. Once the plague had subsided, the task of removing the dead was as gruesome as it was necessary. Butchers were sent in to carry out the dreadful work, dismembering the decomposing bodies and carting them away.

Since then, people have said that Mary's Close transformed into a realm of ghosts, as the spirits of those who perished under such tragic circumstances were not easily put to rest. The story of Thomas Coltheart, a lawyer who lived there later, is one of the most famous. He and his wife saw strange things in their home. They saw the head of an old man with a long beard and scary eyes floating around. Sometimes, a hand appeared, trying to shake Thomas's hand. The sight of a ghostly child hovering in mid-air was pretty common, while deformed phantom animals added to the surreal spectacle.

Yet, it was the spirit of a little girl, discovered by a Japanese medium, that left a profound impact on people. The medium, overwhelmed by a heavy, depressive aura, encountered the ghost of a young girl who had died from the plague. She mourned not only her life but also her lost doll. In response to her sorrow, the television crew and subsequent visitors began leaving gifts for her. Now, a collection of toys, dolls, books, and coins lies in the corner of the room, serving as a tribute to the girl's lost innocence and the tragic history of Mary's Close.

The popular belief that Mary's Close was sealed with plague victims inside in 1645 is a tale that has captivated many. However, there's another side to the story, a view that contradicts this grim narrative and sheds a different light on the history of the close.

Contrary to the belief that the close was a sealed tomb for its plague-ridden residents, historical records suggest that those healthy enough or willing to move were relocated to Burgh Muir, an area outside the city. For those who chose to stay, life in Mary's Close went on, albeit under the dark shadow of the plague. These residents continued their daily routines and even ran their businesses amidst the crisis. Houses affected by the plague were marked with white flags, signaling the need for food and coal. This system allowed council workers and volunteers to provide necessary supplies to those in quarantine.

One figure who played a crucial role during this time was George Rae, a plague doctor known for his visits to Mary's Close. Rae, like other plague doctors of his time, wore a striking and somewhat bizarre outfit. He wore a mask shaped like a crow's beak and was dressed head to toe in leather. The mask was not just for show. The beak was stuffed with herbs and flowers with strong scents, which were thought to keep away the airborne diseases that were believed to spread the plague. In reality, the disease was spread by bacteria, and Rae's leather outfit inadvertently protected him from the bites of fleas that carried the plague.

The mask of a plague doctor.
Juan Antonio Ruiz Rivas, CC BY-SA 3.0 <http://creativecommons.org/licenses/by-sa/3.0/>, via Wikimedia Commons: https://commons.wikimedia.org/wiki/File:Medico_peste.jpg

Rae's methods for treating the plague were as extreme as his appearance. He would cut open the boils of plague victims to drain the pus, then seal the wounds with a red-hot poker. While this technique sounds horrific, it surprisingly saved many lives.

Because of the dangers involved, plague doctors like Rae were promised financial rewards by the city council for their risky, life-saving work. However, when it came time to pay, the council broke their promise, leaving many doctors, including Rae, uncompensated for their efforts. It's believed that Rae never received full payment for his heroic actions and lived out his days without due recognition.

Despite the efforts of Rae and others, many residents of Mary's Close succumbed to the plague. Yet, the close was never sealed off as is often believed. Its history took another turn in the 18th century with the construction of the Royal Exchange. This development led to the demolition and burial of part of the close. It remained accessible, with a few small businesses operating within, including the Cheney family's saw business, which lasted until 1902.

After the Cheney family left, Mary's Close was finally sealed off and forgotten, only to be rediscovered years later during a roadworks project when workers accidentally broke through into the hidden close. During World War II, the close served as a bomb shelter, lying dormant again until the 1990s. It was then that Mary King's Close was reopened as the fascinating tourist attraction we see today, a place that continues to intrigue and haunt visitors with its complex and layered history.

Chapter 6: The Mysterious Creatures of Scottish Folklore

The story begins on a misty evening in a small village nestled not far from the shores of a tranquil loch. There, we find a sad little boy. He had just stormed out of his house following a heated dispute with his mother over his wish to stay at his friend's house for the night. Frustrated and thinking that his mother would never understand him, the little boy decided to calm himself by walking to his favorite spot by the loch.

As soon as he arrived, the boy sat on the boulder by the loch, enjoying the peace that nature offered. Nearly half an hour passed, and he noticed that the sky had begun to turn dark. As he stood up, preparing to make his way home, the little boy saw something he had never seen before in his life.

The surface of the loch stirred, and from the depths emerged a majestic horse. Its coat shimmered like the midnight sea, and its eyes gleamed with an otherworldly light. To the little boy, the mysterious horse appeared not as a beast to fear but as a beautiful creature, inviting him for a ride. The water horse, known as the each-uisge, let out a nicker that echoed like a distant melody, enticing the little boy to come closer. The boy, though wary, felt a strange pull, a curiosity that overrode the cautionary tales he had grown up with. In a moment of boldness or perhaps folly, the innocent little boy reached out and touched the creature, its coat cool and smooth under his fingers.

Sensing no danger, the boy mounted the beast, his face full of excitement, as he had never ridden such a magnificent mount before. But the creature had its own intention. A second later, the each-uisge revealed itself. Its eyes suddenly turned dark as the abyss, and its smooth body began to change, growing slick and wet. Startled by the transformation, the little boy tried to dismount the beast, but both of his hands were stuck to the water horse's wet coat. The boy desperately screamed for help, drawing the attention of a passerby who was returning from the next village, but it was too late.

The each-uisge, with a strength that belied its graceful form, quickly plunged into the depths, dragging the helpless boy with it. The loch churned and roiled as the water horse descended, revealing its true nature as a predator of the deep. The passerby, having witnessed the incident, could do nothing but stand by the shore, his face stricken with horror and trauma as the boy's screams faded into the night.

Legend has it that the each-uisge devoured its victims, leaving nothing but the liver to float to the surface. As the passerby waited with bated breath, a grim sign emerged from the loch: a liver, the last remnant of the poor boy.

From that day forth, the tale of the boy and the each-uisge became a cautionary story passed down through generations. Parents warned their children of the dangers lurking in the depths of the lochs and of the water horse that could charm and deceive, its beauty masking a deadly nature.

The supposed skeleton of an each-uisge displayed in the garden of a house in Ord.
John Allan / Each Uisge Earballach: https://commons.wikimedia.org/wiki/File:Each_Uisge_Earballach_-_geograph.org.uk_-_218481.jpg

Yet, the lochs weren't the only places where caution was advised. The Scots were equally warned of the dangers lurking in streams and rivers; these were the domains of the kelpies. These mystical creatures were capable of transforming from their equine form into human figures, and they have been the subject of many tales. A peculiar characteristic often gave away their true identity: the presence of water weeds in their hair, a subtle hint of their aquatic origins.

One such tale, recounted by the Scottish folklorist Walter Gregor, tells of a kelpie that assumed the form of a wizened old man. This figure was often seen muttering to himself while sitting on a bridge, deeply focused on stitching a pair of trousers. His presence, which was eerie and out of place, aroused suspicion among the locals. One day, a passerby, convinced that the old man was a kelpie in disguise, struck him on the head. The blow caused the kelpie to revert to its true form, and it quickly scampered away to the safety of its lair in a nearby pond.

Other accounts of kelpies in human form are more sinister. Some describe a rough, shaggy man who would leap behind a lone traveler, gripping and crushing him. Others speak of kelpies tearing apart and devouring their human victims.

A particular folktale from Barra, an island off the coast of Scotland, offers a different perspective on the nature of kelpies. This story revolves around a lonely kelpie that transformed itself into a handsome young man, hoping to woo a young girl and make her his wife. However, the sharp and observant girl recognized the young man for what he truly was. While he slept, she removed his silver necklace, which was actually his bridle, causing him to revert back to his horse form.

The Kelpies, thirty-meter-high sculptures in Grangemouth depicting the mythical creatures. © User:Colin / Wikimedia Commons: https://commons.wikimedia.org/wiki/File:The_Kelpies_1-1_Stitch.jpg

Instead of fearing the kelpie, the girl saw an opportunity. She took the transformed kelpie back to her father's farm, where she put it to work for a full year. At the year's end, she rode the kelpie to consult a wise man. Following the wise man's advice, she returned the silver necklace to the kelpie, which allowed him to regain his human form.

The wise man then posed a question to the kelpie: would he choose to remain a kelpie or become a mortal man? The kelpie, in turn, asked the girl if she would agree to be his wife were he a man. When she confirmed she would, the kelpie, without hesitation, made the choice to become mortal. The story ends with their marriage, a union that transformed the once-lonely and potentially malevolent kelpie into a loving husband, illustrating the transformative power of love and understanding.

This tale of the kelpie diverges from the more common narratives of an evil creature, offering a glimpse into the complexity of these mythical creatures. It suggests that beneath their fearsome exterior, there may be a longing for connection, understanding, and perhaps redemption, themes that resonate deeply in the rich folklore of Scotland.

The Legendary Loch Ness Monster

Loch Ness is an expansive body of water, stretching over 22 square miles and plunging to depths of over 750 feet. It is not just one of Scotland's largest lochs by volume but also a treasure trove of ancient myths and legends. Its most famous inhabitant, the Loch Ness Monster, affectionately known as Nessie, has captured the world's imagination.

Loch Ness, Scotland's largest loch by volume.
Sam Fentress, CC BY-SA 2.0 <https://creativecommons.org/licenses/by-sa/2.0>, via Wikimedia Commons: https://commons.wikimedia.org/wiki/File:LochNessUrquhart.jpg

The legend of Nessie dates back to ancient times, with the first recorded sighting attributed to the revered Irish missionary Saint Columba in 565 CE.

As the story goes, Saint Columba was traveling through the Scottish Highlands, spreading the Christian faith among the Pictish tribes. His journey brought him to the shores of Loch Ness.

One day, as Columba and his companions were near the loch, they came upon a group of locals burying a man by the water's edge. They inquired about what had happened and were shocked by the tragic tale. The man had been swimming in the loch when he was suddenly attacked and killed by a monstrous creature that lurked in its depths. The locals spoke of the beast with a mix of fear and awe, describing it as a creature unlike any other, a terror of the deep that had claimed the lives of many.

Undeterred by the grim stories, Saint Columba was determined to cross the loch. He instructed one of his followers, a man named Lugne Mocumin, to swim across the water and bring back a boat from the other side. As Lugne obediently plunged into the dark, cold waters, a sense of dread fell over the onlookers, for they knew the beast lay hidden below.

True to their fears, as Lugne swam, the waters of the loch began to churn. From the depths emerged the monstrous creature, its great head and long neck surging toward the defenseless swimmer. The onlookers cried out in terror, certain that Lugne would meet the same fate as the man they had just buried. But Saint Columba stood firm on the shore, showing no sign of fear. Instead, he raised his hand and, with a powerful voice, invoked the name of God, commanding the beast, "Go no further. Do not touch the man. Go back at once." To the amazement of all, the creature halted as if struck by an invisible force. It then turned and disappeared back into the depths of the loch, leaving Lugne unharmed.

Unless one is a true believer of Nessie, it is easy to see this as a tale made up to symbolize the power of faith and the triumph of good over the unseen evils of the world. Over the centuries, the legend of Nessie grew, with the mysterious depths of Loch Ness providing the perfect backdrop for the creature's elusive nature. The ancient Picts, known for their intricate stone carvings, depicted a mysterious beast with flippers, suggesting that belief in such a creature has been a part of local culture for millennia.

Swedish naturalist Bengt Sjogren proposed that Nessie's legend might be linked to kelpie myths, suggesting a shared origin in Scottish folklore. However, others believe Nessie is a separate being altogether. Unlike the shape-shifting kelpies, Nessie is often described as a giant sea serpent, stirring the waters of Loch Ness with its movements.

Eyewitness accounts of Nessie vary, but a common description is that of a massive creature with two or three humps protruding above the water's surface. However, these sightings have been met with much skepticism. Experts suggest that such observations could be optical illusions, possibly caused by boat wakes on the loch's surface or even by birds or other wildlife.

The most widely accepted depiction of Nessie is that of a plesiosaur, a prehistoric marine reptile. This image was popularized by several notable sightings and photographs. In 1934, Arthur Grant, a veterinary student, claimed to have a close encounter with the creature, describing it as having a long neck and a small head. This account was soon followed by the infamous "Surgeon's Photograph," which appears to show Nessie with a long neck and small head, like a plesiosaur.

A drawing of Nessie by Arthur Grant.
https://commons.wikimedia.org/wiki/File:Arthur_Grant_loch_ness_sketch.png

However, this theory presents several issues. Loch Ness was formed after the last ice age, so it would have been uninhabitable by a prehistoric reptile like the plesiosaur. Furthermore, as a reptile, such a creature would need to surface frequently for air, leading to the expectation of more frequent sightings than have been reported.

Despite these challenges, the legend of Nessie continues to be a symbol of mystery and fascination. The story of the Loch Ness Monster transcends the realm of folklore and has become a cultural phenomenon. It draws thousands of visitors to Loch Ness each year, with people hoping to catch a glimpse of the elusive creature.

The allure of Nessie lies not just in the mystery of its existence but also in the human fascination with the unknown. The Loch Ness

Monster embodies the unexplained and the undiscovered, fueling our imagination and inviting endless speculation and debate.

So, it is no surprise that the legend of Nessie has evolved over the years, with numerous hoaxes and scientific expeditions adding layers to the story. From sonar scans to underwater photography, efforts to prove or disprove Nessie's existence have only heightened the intrigue. Each unexplained sighting or blurry photograph adds to the lore, keeping the legend alive in the hearts and minds of believers and skeptics alike.

Redcaps

Redcaps, also known as powries or dunters, are said to be small, stout, and incredibly strong creatures. They dwell in the ruined castles and towers along the Scottish Borders. These beings, as described by 19th-century folklorist William Henderson, are among the most sinister in Scottish folklore.

Redcaps are, of course, characterized by their red caps. These caps are central to their very existence. The caps are dyed in human blood, which the redcaps are compelled to replenish by committing murder. Should the blood in the cap dry up, it is believed that the redcap would die.

These creatures are often depicted as old, wiry men with long, sharp talons and teeth. Their eyes gleam with a malevolent light, and they wear iron boots that clank ominously as they move. Redcaps are swift and merciless. They are known for their brutality and for haunting the sites of tyranny and bloodshed.

One of the most famous tales of the murderous redcaps took place in a dark, dilapidated castle in the Scottish Borders. This castle, once a site of great battles, had become the perfect abode for a redcap. In the tale, a wandering traveler seeking shelter for the night stumbled upon the castle. Unaware of its sinister inhabitant, he entered, looking for a place to rest. As night fell, the castle's eerie silence was broken by the sound of heavy, iron-clad footsteps. The traveler, filled with dread, quickly rose to his feet and hid in the shadows, watching in horror as the redcap appeared.

The creature was indeed grotesque, with twisted features and a cap soaked in fresh blood. Its eyes glowed as it scoured the castle for its next victim. The traveler, realizing the grave danger he was in, knew he must escape before he was spotted.

As the redcap approached his hiding place, the traveler remembered a piece of lore he had heard in his travels: redcaps could be repelled by words of scripture or by the cross. With no cross in hand, he recited verses from the Bible he had learned in his youth. As he spoke the sacred words, the redcap let out a furious howl and recoiled as if struck by an unseen force. Seizing the opportunity, the traveler fled the castle without ever looking back despite the sounds of the redcap's enraged screams echoing behind him. He ran through the night, not stopping until the castle was far behind him.

The most well-known story is about Robin Redcap, the most notorious redcap, and his connection with Lord William de Soulis. Lord William, a 13th-century nobleman, was infamous for his brutal rule and involvement in black magic. He was widely feared and despised throughout the Scottish Borders for his extreme cruelty. He lived in the ominous Hermitage Castle, which we talked about in a previous chapter.

According to legend, Lord Soulis was not alone in his nefarious activities. He had a companion by his side, a redcap named Robin. Unlike the common redcaps known for haunting dilapidated castles, Robin Redcap was bound to Lord Soulis, serving as his familiar and aiding in his dark rituals. His cap was often drenched in the blood of his lord's victims, and he was said to possess strength far greater than his size would suggest.

The locals believed that Lord Soulis and Robin Redcap engaged in abominable acts, including the abduction and sacrifice of children. The pair's reign of terror reached a peak with a dark scheme in which Lord Soulis, with Robin Redcap's help, sought to bind the dark forces to his will.

The local populace decided to put an end to Lord Soulis's tyranny. Legend has it that the local wise men, knowing that neither steel nor rope could kill a warlock, captured Lord Soulis and boiled him alive in a cauldron at Ninestane Rig. As for Robin Redcap, his evil spirit was said to have vanished into thin air after the death of his master.

The ghost of Sir William de Soulis is said to still haunt the corridors of Hermitage Castle. Visitors to the castle have reported eerie occurrences, with some claiming to hear the heart-rending sobs of children echoing through the crumbling corridors.

It is said that Robin's malevolent spirit also still lingers in the ruins of Hermitage Castle. Visitors to the castle have reported feeling an ominous presence, and some claim to have seen a small, wizened figure with a blood-red cap quietly watching them from the shadows.

Selkies

In the pantheon of Scottish mythological creatures, the selkies hold a unique place. Unlike the brutal kelpies or the sinister redcaps, selkies are known for their kind and benevolent nature. They are said to have aided children and fishermen lost at sea.

These gentle creatures of the sea are known for their ability to transform and for their mesmerizing singing voices. Their songs, often heard along the shores and cliffs of the Orkney and Shetland Islands, are said to be so captivating that they can soothe the restless sea and enchant anyone who hears them.

In Scottish lore, the selkie's ability to shift between seal and human form is closely connected to their seal skin. A selkie must carefully guard their precious skin; without it, they are unable to return to their original form. If a selkie's skin is lost or stolen, they will be bound to the land and unable to return to the sea. When selkies are in their human form, they are famous for their extraordinary beauty and elegance, often captivating the hearts of those who encounter them.

A depiction of selkies on a stamp originating from the Faroe Islands.
https://commons.wikimedia.org/wiki/File:Faroese_stamp_579_the_seal_woman.jpg

The most well-known tale about the selkies is the touching story of "The Selkie Bride." This tale begins with a lonely fisherman who lived by the sea. He spent his days watching the seals along the shore, but he was particularly drawn to one beautiful selkie who would shed her skin and bask in the sun.

One evening, driven by a desire for companionship, the fisherman stealthily approached the selkie while she was in human form and stole her seal skin. Without it, she could not return to the sea. The fisherman, overcome with love and longing, begged her to stay and be his wife. And so, the selkie, unable to return to her home without her skin, reluctantly agreed.

They lived together for many years, and the selkie bride bore the fisherman several children. Although she was a loving wife and mother, a part of her always yearned for the sea. Her heart ached for her true home, and she would often gaze longingly at the ocean for hours, dreaming and reminiscing about her life beneath the waves.

One day, one of her children discovered a seal skin in their home. Not realizing its significance, the child brought it to her mother. Overwhelmed with both joy and sadness, the selkie knew she had to make a difficult choice. That evening, as the sun dipped below the horizon, she kissed her children goodbye, donned her seal skin, and returned to the sea.

The fisherman eventually returned to find his wife gone. He searched the shore in vain, calling her name repeatedly, but she was nowhere to be found. From that day forward, he would often see a seal watching him from the waves, its eyes reflecting a deep understanding and love. The fisherman knew it was his beloved selkie bride, watching over him and their children from her home in the sea.

While many stories of selkies feature female beings, male selkies also occupy a significant place in Scottish folklore. Male selkies are often portrayed as irresistible to mortal women, especially those who are unhappy or longing for their husbands who have gone to sea. Legends say that male selkies are particularly drawn to married women who yearn for something beyond their mundane lives.

According to legend, if a woman wishes to summon a male selkie, she must weep seven tears into the sea. This act of sorrow and longing is said to call forth a selkie man from the depths of the ocean. He will then offer the love and companionship she truly desires.

The lore surrounding selkies is rich and varied. Some stories suggest that selkies can only shed their skins and take on human form once every seven years. This limitation adds a sense of fleeting magic and rarity to their interactions with humans. Other tales hint at a more mystical origin for the selkies. Some believe that selkies were once humans who committed sinful acts and were transformed as a punishment. Others view them as fallen angels, creatures of divine beauty and grace that do not quite belong to either the world of humans or the realm of the divine.

Despite all these different interpretations of selkie tales, the themes of transformation and longing are always present. Selkies, whether seen as magical creatures or as humans cursed to live in two worlds, represent the timeless desire for connection, freedom, and the exploration of one's true nature.

Chapter 7: Witchcraft, Dark Magic, and Curses

Centuries ago, in a small village on the east of Scotland, lived a man who had been plagued by a series of unfortunate events. He had lost his mother the previous winter, followed by his only son the next spring. To make matters worse, his crops failed, and his livestock grew sickly. It appeared as though the misfortunes followed him day and night, casting a dark shadow over his life.

As the days turned into months, the man's melancholy only deepened. He watched as his once-prosperous life crumbled around him. But there was one constant presence in his life, the woman who had stood by his side through thick and thin—his wife. She had been a source of comfort and solace in his darkest hours.

However, grief can be a poison that distorts one's thoughts and perceptions. The man's grief began to turn into suspicion, and he grew increasingly paranoid. He noticed that his wife would occasionally slip out of their quiet cottage at night, leaving him alone in the darkness. His mind raced with thoughts of betrayal and deceit, and he started to believe that his wife was involved in dark deeds.

One day, he confided in his neighbors, voicing his suspicions to them in hushed tones. They, too, had noticed his wife's nighttime wanderings and began to share his apprehension. Rumors spread like wildfire through the village, and before long, everyone believed that the man's wife was a witch, practicing dark magic under the secret of night.

The man's accusations became louder and more insistent. He proclaimed to anyone who would listen that his wife was a witch, capable of cursing the land and causing misfortune. By this time, it was clear that his grief had driven him to madness, and he couldn't see the truth. His wife was merely seeking solace in the stillness of the night to try to ease her own worries and sadness.

The villagers, swayed by the man's relentless accusations, gathered on one fateful evening and confronted the accused woman. She pleaded her innocence, tears streaming down her cheeks, her voice breaking, but her protests fell on deaf ears. Fear and hysteria had taken hold of the villagers, and they wanted to rid their community of the supposed witch.

In a chaotic and somber ceremony, the woman was banished from the village, the only home she had ever known. The woman looked at his husband, hoping he would come to her defense, yet his eyes showed no remorse. It was as if he was disgusted by her very presence. And so, she left, heartbroken and alone, disappearing into the dense woods with nowhere else to go and no one to turn to. What happened to her afterward remained a mystery. Some claimed she eventually managed to rebuild her life far from the village that condemned her, but she no longer knew how to smile or laugh. Others suggested that she met her demise in the woods, perhaps killed by wild beasts that roamed the area.

In the folklore of the Scottish people, magic was seen as a mix of both good and evil. They believed in kind fairies and spirits that could bring luck and happiness, but they also harbored a strong fear of witchcraft and its potential for harm.

In the Middle Ages, when superstitions ran rampant, women were often the targets of accusations of witchcraft. This was partly due to societal norms, as women were seen as having a closer connection to the mystical and the unknown compared to men. Their roles as healers and midwives made them susceptible to suspicion, and their knowledge of herbs and remedies sometimes fueled accusations of witchcraft.

Witchcraft in Scotland was characterized by the use of black magic to bring harm to others. Witches were believed to have obtained their powers either through initiation into a coven or through inheritance. They were seen as agents of the devil, practitioners of evil, and purveyors of malevolent spells.

One of the most chilling aspects of witchcraft was the belief that witches could use personal items, such as hair, nail clippings, clothing, or even bodily waste, to work their dark magic against their targets. This belief was not unique only to Scotland; it was common in other parts of the world, including in Europe, Africa, South Asia, Polynesia, Melanesia, and North and South America. Another one of the sinister claims involving dark magic was that some witches would murder innocent children to obtain ingredients for their spells.

Conditions that we now recognize as postpartum psychosis were often mistaken for signs of witchcraft or black magic back in the medieval era. Because of this, women who displayed symptoms of mental distress or erratic behavior were sometimes accused of consorting with dark forces and the devil himself.

Witches were also believed to work in secret, often gathering at night when normal humans were sleeping. However, witches were said to be the most vulnerable while sleeping. They were also thought to transgress social norms by engaging in practices like cannibalism, incest, and open nudity. Some even claimed that witches had associations with certain animals, suggesting they could shape-shift into these creatures or had animal helpers to aid them in completing their sinister work.

Necromancy, the darkest of all black magic practices, was also attributed to witches. It involved communicating with the dead and summoning dark spirits. It was a terrifying idea that struck fear into the hearts of many.

However, it was possible to seek protection from the malicious powers of these evil witches. Referred to as "cunning folks," these special individuals were believed to possess the ability to cast protective spells. They were often sought after, especially if one wished to thwart a certain dark magic intended to harm them. Typically, charms, talismans, and amulets were the most common items used to safeguard themselves from witchcraft. Anti-witch marks, inscribed symbols or patterns, were sometimes carved into buildings to ward off evil magic. Witch bottles, which contained things like pins and urine, were buried to turn away curses. Additionally, items like horse skulls were sometimes concealed within the walls of buildings as protective symbols.

Once a person was sure they had been put under a witch's spell or a curse, they sought various means of release. Apart from consulting with the cunning folks, some believed that another cure for bewitchment was to persuade or force the alleged witch to lift their spell. However, in darker times, people attempted to thwart witchcraft by physically punishing the accused. Banishment, wounding, torture, and even execution were seen as ways to cleanse the community of this perceived evil.

This atmosphere of fear and paranoia led to a period in history known as the witch hunts. Many individuals, mostly women, were accused of witchcraft and subjected to trials that often ended in death. A majority of the time, accusations of witchcraft were a convenient scapegoat for any inconvenience or misfortune troubling a community. When plagues, diseases, famines, or other calamities struck, people pointed their fingers at supposed witches, blaming them for the afflictions and labeling them as agents of the devil.

The witch hunts in Scotland were a dark and troubling chapter in its history, marked by fear, paranoia, and the persecution of hundreds of innocent people. The roots of the Scottish witch hunts can be traced back to the reign of King James V.

As a young boy, King James V had been imprisoned by his stepfather, Archibald Douglas, 6th Earl of Angus. His escape from captivity left him with a burning desire for vengeance, not only against Douglas but also against his extended family, including his sister, Janet Douglas, Lady Glamis. In 1537, James arrested Janet, accusing her of witchcraft and concocting potions in a conspiracy to kill him.

The charges against Janet were largely founded on rumors and the desire for revenge. Even those who knew her were not safe; they were tortured mercilessly and forced to voice out any so-called evidence that could cement Janet's downfall. On July 17th, 1537, in a tragic and brutal event, Janet Douglas was burned alive on Castle Hill in Edinburgh, with her own son forced to watch the terrifying scene.

This event marked the beginning of a dark era in Scotland's history, where accusations of witchcraft became increasingly common and often led to gruesome outcomes. The paranoia surrounding witchcraft never subsided; instead, it only intensified as the years went by.

One of the most notorious episodes in the Scottish witch trials was the North Berwick witch trials in the late 16th century. King James VI, who was deeply superstitious and considered himself the devil's greatest mortal enemy, personally examined the accused individuals. He even wrote a book on the subject called *Daemonologie*, which further fueled the hysteria surrounding witchcraft.

An illustration of a witch trial in the 19th century.
https://commons.wikimedia.org/wiki/File:Punishment_of_Witches.png

In the North Berwick witch trials, a group of people, mainly women from East Lothian, were accused of meeting with the devil and conspiring to conjure storms that would kill King James VI and his wife, Queen Anne, upon their return from Denmark. As per usual, the accused were subjected to harsh interrogations and brutal torture, including sleep deprivation and other forms of torment, to extract confessions.

Women accused of witchcraft kneeling before King James during the North Berwick witch trials.
https://commons.wikimedia.org/wiki/File:North_Berwick_Witches.png

No one could live in peace during this traumatic time, not even the most innocent of all. The mere presence of birthmarks or unusual physical characteristics was often considered evidence of witchcraft. Many individuals were captured, tried, and executed under the suspicion of being witches.

Another notable witch hunt was the Great Scottish witch hunt of 1649-1650. The years leading up to this dark episode were far from peaceful. The people of Scotland were torn apart by religious and political conflicts and were deeply affected by the Wars of the Three Kingdoms. This turbulent atmosphere created fertile ground for accusations of witchcraft.

It was common to see people pointing fingers at each other, claiming they had made pacts with the devil and were capable of wielding dark powers to bring harm to their already distraught community. Fear and suspicion ran rampant. Families and friends were torn apart, as mistrust greatly festered in the hearts of the people.

To seek out these perceived threats, the Scottish Parliament appointed special commissioners known as "witch prickers." These individuals claimed to have the uncanny ability to identify witches through physical examinations. Oftentimes, they would meticulously examine the accused person's body for any unusual skin blemishes, moles, birthmarks, or other marks that they believed could be marks of the devil. Any irregularity in the skin could be interpreted as evidence of witchcraft. Witch prickers also used various sharp objects, such as needles, pins, or bodkins, to prick the accused person's skin. They believed that the devil's mark would be insensitive to pain and would not bleed when pricked.

Once accused, it was only a matter of seconds before unspeakable horrors took place. Sleep deprivation, binding, and even the dreaded "swimming" tests were used. In the swimming test, the accused would be stripped to their undergarments and bound, with their right thumb tied to their left big toe and their left thumb tied to their right big toe, to prevent them from swimming. They would then be lowered into a body of water. If the accused floated, they were deemed witches, as it was believed that the pure element of water rejected them due to their connection with the devil, and their fate was sealed. If they sank, they were considered innocent because the water had accepted them. However, they often met a tragic end beneath the water's surface if not rescued in time.

Religious leaders also played a significant role in fanning the flames of the witch hunts. A new Witchcraft Act was passed in 1649. Some ministers and clergymen preached sermons that reinforced the belief in witchcraft and the need to eradicate it. The religious fervor of the time only served to heighten the hysteria surrounding witch trials.

The Great Scottish witch hunt of 1649-1650 resulted in a significant number of executions. It is estimated that over three hundred individuals, mostly women of low social status, met their fate as witches during this dark period.

As time passed, the political landscape shifted, and the authorities turned their focus elsewhere. By the mid-1650s, the clamor for witch trials began to subside, though there were occasional local outbreaks from time to time. One tragic case that stands out during this period is that of Lilias Adie from the town of Torryburn in 1704. Accused of witchcraft, Lilias was subjected to brutal interrogation and torture. The relentless pressure eventually led her to confess to having interactions with the devil, attending meetings with other witches, and even engaging in carnal relations with the devil himself. The authorities pressed her to reveal the names of the other witches, but Lilias died before she could stand trial.

Since Lilias died before being formally convicted, her body could not be subjected to the gruesome fate of burning at the stake. However, the community remained convinced of her guilt and feared that the devil might reanimate her corpse. To prevent this, Lilias was buried in a peculiar manner—between the high and low tide marks on the beach, a place neither entirely land nor sea. A heavy stone slab was then added to her grave to ensure that her restless spirit would never get the chance to rise from the underworld.

The last recorded witch executions in Scotland occurred in 1706. The last trial took place in 1727. However, these dark episodes of unjust trials are never forgotten; instead, they serve as a somber lesson in history.

Acknowledging the wrongs done to those accused of being witches, the Scottish government formally apologized in 2022. Several memorials have been erected in remembrance of the victims. At Edinburgh Castle's esplanade, one can find the Witches Well, a monument to those who suffered during the witch hunts. The Fife Witches Trail also acts as a moving reminder of the stories and lives tragically altered by the fear and hysteria surrounding witchcraft.

Curses in Scottish Folktales

Although the old witch hunts are now part of history, the fear of curses remains for some people. Curses are thought to be spoken by powerful individuals, usually driven by emotions like anger, betrayal, or a wish for revenge. These curses are thought to hold the power to shape destinies, influence the future, and bring calamity upon those who invite their wrath.

The belief in curses often revolves around the idea that negative energy can be channeled through words or rituals, causing misfortune to befall the cursed individual or their descendants. Some curses are said to linger for generations, casting a shadow over entire families or even communities. One such story took place in the village of Lochbuie. This tale, recorded by the Scottish folklorist John Gregorson Campbell, tells the story of sisters, secrets, and the power of a curse.

According to the story, the older sister stood out for her beauty and kindness. Her charm and warmth drew the admiration of many, earning her the name Lovely Mairearad. Her sister, Ailsa, was smaller in size, though she possessed the same kindness as her elder sister. However, it was her ultimate devotion to Mairearad that earned Ailsa her nickname; she was often called by the villagers as Limpet Ailsa.

One day, a cheeky lad and his group of friends walked by and pestered Limpet Ailsa about Lovely Mairearad's affections. His endless questions pushed Ailsa to the brink, and she snapped, "My sister has a fairy lover, more handsome than any of you!" Laughter immediately erupted, but Ailsa, filled with annoyance, challenged them to visit their cottage at dusk.

The lads, drawn by the promise of entertainment, followed Ailsa. To their amazement, a real fairy appeared. The birds stopped singing, and the clouds stood still. Knowing the mortals had discovered him, he vanished as quickly as he appeared, leaving them in complete awe. Yet, Lovely Mairearad's response shattered their joy. She wailed, having warned Ailsa never to reveal her secret lest she be abandoned by her fairy lover.

From that day, Mairearad became a wandering soul, shunning houses and kind words. Desperate villagers tried to reconcile the two sisters, but all they heard were Mairearad's cruel curses, foretelling revenge upon Ailsa's descendants:

"If a fae indeed possesses an otherworldly power, get me my revenge, but may it be on her descendants."

Limpet Ailsa spent a year trying to mend their bond but had no success. She retreated to the north of the isle, where she married and had a son named Torquil, who inherited Mairearad's beauty and charm. Torquil possessed more than just his fair appearance; he was also known for his exceptional reaping skills. Some claimed he could reap as much as seven men could. Oftentimes, he would challenge the villagers during harvest time, boasting his talent as the best reaper in the area.

However, one day, a lady caught Torquil's attention. This mysterious woman, known among the villagers as the Maiden of the Cairn, possessed a reaping skill that matched Torquil's. Of course, Torquil, in his youthful pride, felt challenged by the mysterious lady. Thus, he picked up his sickle and joined her in the field, convinced that he could easily outdo her.

But as they toiled side by side, Torquil soon realized that the Maiden was no ordinary woman. She seemed to glide through the stalks of grain, her sickle moving with an otherworldly grace. Torquil struggled to keep up. His legs trembled, and his chest heaved with exhaustion.

Suddenly, in the midst of their reaping contest, the Maiden spoke words of warning.

"It is an evil thing, early on Monday, to reap the harvest maiden."

According to Scottish beliefs, the harvest maiden is a special doll, a representation of the last bundle of grain that marks the end of the harvest season in Scotland. But Torquil, in his eagerness, made a grave mistake. He cut the harvest maiden too soon. This act was seen as bad luck. It angered the spirits and magical beings believed to protect the crops. They took offense and unleashed their wrath upon Torquil.

And so, Torquil's life ended in the very field he aimed to conquer. The Maiden vanished, and Mairearad's wish, or rather curse, came true—her sister's family met a tragic end.

Of course, the world of curses is not confined to the distant past. Sometimes, it creeps into our lives, even in more recent times. Another chilling story took place sometime in the 1930s. It began with a well-respected Scottish baronet named Sir Alexander Seton and his wife, who embarked on a journey to Egypt, a land rich with ancient mysteries.

Their Egyptian adventure was said to have led them to the Temple of Luxor. Despite the strict prohibition against removing anything from the sacred tombs, Lady Seton could not resist the temptation. She quietly plucked a small bone as a memento, a token of their exotic travels, and brought it back to their grand home in Learmonth Gardens, Edinburgh. This mysterious—or rather cursed—piece of bone was displayed in a glass case stored in their lavish dining room. This seemingly innocent act inadvertently set in motion a series of events they would soon come to regret.

Upon their return, strange and unsettling occurrences began to unfold. Mysterious crashes reverberated through the house, and furniture was discovered in disarray as if moved by unseen hands. Ornaments lay shattered in rooms that had been empty mere moments before. Lady Seton herself fell suddenly and inexplicably ill, her ailment baffling even the most skilled doctors.

Time and time again, the family found themselves besieged by bizarre happenings that defied all explanation. But the most unsettling of all was the apparition that manifested itself in the house—an eerie figure cloaked in long robes. This ghostly presence appeared before multiple witnesses, both residents and visitors alike. The house's servants, overwhelmed by fear, desperately sought employment elsewhere, unwilling to endure the unnerving atmosphere another day.

In an attempt to rid themselves of this curse, Sir Alexander lent the bone to a scientist friend. To their astonishment, the ghostly disturbances ceased at Learmonth Gardens but resurfaced in the home of the scientist. The haunting stories soon reached the crowds, attracting the attention of even the newspapers of Edinburgh, which later dubbed the ghostly disturbances as the "The Curse of the Pharaoh."

In a bid to relieve his friend from the torment, Sir Alexander Seton reclaimed the bone and returned it to Learmonth Gardens. Once more, the house seemed to come alive with inexplicable phenomena. Even Sir Alexander himself fell ill.

In the end, seeking solace and deliverance, Sir Alexander turned to a priest. The bone was unearthed, and in a ritual of purifying fire, it was reduced to ashes. With the bone's destruction, the curse was finally lifted, and the tormented house was freed from its malevolent grip.

Chapter 8: Love and Betrayal: The Sagas of Scotland

In addition to stories of magical creatures and malicious beings intervening in the lives of mortals, Scottish folklore is deeply cherished for its love stories and sagas. These tales, which often weaved together the themes of beauty, tragedy, and destiny, strike a chord with the Scots, reflecting their fondness for stories that mirror the complexities of the human heart and the dramatic landscapes that surround them. One such tale that was passed from one generation to the next is that of Deirdre, set during the reign of Conchobar, the king of Ulster.

It began in Ireland when the king attended a feast at the house of Felimid the Harper. Amidst the celebration, an incident occurred that led the druid Cathbad to make a prophecy about Felimid's unborn daughter, Deirdre. Cathbad foretold that Deirdre would grow up to be a woman of unparalleled beauty. Felimid and his wife were overjoyed upon hearing this, but their expressions immediately changed when the druid made another remark.

"But anything excessive never brings good. True, your daughter will be the fairest of all, but her life will also be marked by tragedy and sorrow. Our people will soon be divided. Brothers will fight each other, hoping they can win dear Deirdre's affection."

Upon listening to Cathbad's words, the men of the Red Branch, the elite warriors of Ulster, feared the chaos Deirdre's beauty might bring and demanded that the child be killed. However, King Conchobar, who always desired to be seen as a wise and merciful ruler, refused. He declared that he would take the child upon her birth and raise her in secret. If she did grow into the beauty Cathbad predicted, Conchobar declared that he would marry her, placing her in a position so high that no man would dare look upon her.

And so, true to the prophecy, Deirdre was born with a beauty that promised to eclipse all others. And just as Conchobar had planned, she was placed under the care of a nurse named Leabharcham and hidden away in a secluded valley, far from the prying eyes of the world. There, Deirdre grew up under Leabharcham's protective watch, completely isolated from the outside world. Conchobar was curious about his future bride and made periodic visits to check on her. No one else was allowed to see Deirdre except an old man who tended to the valley. However, the old man was mute, so the secret of her existence remained safe.

The tale took a dramatic turn one fateful day. As Deirdre neared womanhood, an incident sparked a deep longing in her heart. Leabharcham had the old man slaughter a calf. The calf's blood spilled on the snow, drawing a raven to the scene. Deirdre, who had been watching the incident from a close distance, was said to be overly captivated by the contrast of the raven's black feathers against the blood-red snow and the pure white ground. This moment led to a sudden realization. She proclaimed that she would fall in love only with a man who had hair as black as the raven's feathers, skin as white as the pure snow, and cheeks as red as the blood on the snow.

Longing for love, Deirdre asked her caretaker if she knew any man who fit her description. Leabharcham was hesitant at first, but she could never ignore Deirdre for too long. The protective caretaker informed her of one particular man who went by the name Naoise. However, Leabharcham strictly warned her to only observe the man from a distance. After all, he was one of the three sons of Uisneach, who were renowned warriors of high status. Deirdre was raised to believe that she was a commoner. Such a union could attract significant attention and potential danger.

An early 20th-century painting of Deirdre.
https://commons.wikimedia.org/wiki/File:Deirdr%C3%AA,_A_Book_of_Myths.jpg

Deirdre agreed to this. So, one day, she hid amidst the bushes, eyeing Naoise and his brothers from afar. The moment she laid eyes on the man, Deirdre knew he was the embodiment of her heart's desire. Enthralled, she completely forgot about her promise. She leaped out of her hiding spot and confronted Naoise, pleading for him to run away with her. Naoise, who knew that Deirdre was supposed to marry King Conchobar, initially refused her request, but Deirdre already had a plan in mind. She put a geis—a compelling magical vow—on Naoise, binding him to her will.

Deirdre and Naoise, along with his brothers, fled to Scotland. They lived a secluded life deep in the woods, away from the eyes of the world and especially the Ulster king, who was furious with their elopement.

Naoise and his brothers swore service under the Scottish king, but Deirdre soon realized the king coveted her for himself. Knowing that he could not kill the brothers outright, the Scottish king placed the brothers on the front lines of every battle, hoping they would eventually fall. However, their prowess as warriors kept them safe. Deirdre, seeing the danger, persuaded Naoise to flee farther into the wilderness. They eventually settled on a remote island near the training school of the warrior woman Scathach and lived there for many years.

Back in the Ulster capital, Emain Macha, Fergus Mac Roich, a noble of the Red Branch, was the only one brave enough to speak of the sons of Uisneach to Conchobar. Despite Conchobar's rage whenever Naoise's betrayal was mentioned, Fergus, who was fond of the brothers, argued tirelessly for their forgiveness. Eventually, Conchobar relented, allowing Fergus to invite them back under his protection.

So, without delay, Fergus journeyed to Scotland and shared the joyous news with the brothers. They were thrilled at the prospect of returning to Emain Macha and swore an oath not to eat or sleep until they were home. However, during the voyage back, Deirdre grieved for the Scottish lands she had grown to love, singing a lament for the mountains and lochs that had been her haven.

Unbeknownst to Fergus and the brothers, King Conchobar was not ready to let the past go. Fergus Mac Roich had long been under a geis, where he was prohibited from refusing an invitation to a feast of ale. King Conchobar was aware of this vulnerability, and he cunningly invited Fergus to a drinking session, forcing him to abandon his duty to protect Deirdre and the sons of Uisneach. Deirdre, already anxious about their return to Ulster, grew increasingly wary. She implored Fergus not to desert them, accusing him of cowardice for abandoning the men under his protection. Unfortunately, bound by his geis, Fergus had no choice but to attend the feast. He did, however, entrust the safety of Deirdre and the sons of Uisneach to his son Fiachu before departing.

So, the journey continued. Upon reaching Emain Macha, they were greeted not by King Conchobar but by Leabharcham, Deirdre's former caretaker. Ever protective of Deirdre, Leabharcham advised Naoise to hide Deirdre's beauty from prying eyes, hoping none would notice her return. Conchobar, still struggling with his feelings for Deirdre, eventually inquired about her appearance. Leabharcham chose to lie to the king, describing her as a haggard shadow of her former self.

Initially, Conchobar believed Leabharcham's words, and his jealousy waned, replaced by a desire to reintegrate the sons of Uisneach into his service. However, he soon doubted Leabharcham's claim, as he knew the caretaker would do anything to shield her ward from harm. So, to discover the truth, the king sent a spy to ascertain Deirdre's true appearance. Once the spy returned, he confirmed that Deirdre remained the most beautiful woman in Ireland. Conchobar's jealousy and anger were reignited, leading him to order an attack against Naoise and his brothers.

The Red Branch hesitated. While some obeyed the king, others refused to turn against their former comrades. Nevertheless, a battle took place. In the ensuing chaos, Fiachu Mac Roigh, son of Fergus, fought bravely against Conchobar Mac Neasa's son in single combat. Fiachu fell during the duel, and Conchobar's son met his demise soon afterward.

Seeing his men faltering, Conchobar sought the aid of Cathbad the druid. Cathbad agreed to help under one condition: Conchobar was to promise not to kill the sons of Uisneach. Conchobar agreed, declaring he only sought an apology from Naoise. Thus, with the druid's help, the tide of the battle turned. However, Conchobar, bound by his promise to Cathbad, used Maigne Rough Hand, the son of the king of Norway, to execute his vengeance. In the end, Naoise and his brothers met their fate; all three were beheaded by Maigne Rough Hand.

Upon learning that she would never see the love of her life ever again, Deidre immediately plunged into despair. She refused Conchobar's advances despite his attempts to court her with wealth and status. After a year of her steadfast refusal, Conchobar grew irritated. So, he devised a cruel plan. He first asked Deirdre who she despised more than him, to which she replied, Maigne Rough Hand, Naoise's killer. Seizing on this, Conchobar decided to give Deirdre to Maigne for a year, suggesting that Maigne could do anything he wished to her.

"Let's see if you change your mind about me once he gets his hands on you," Conchobar said.

Deirdre was sent away in Maigne's chariot. However, Deirdre had one last act of defiance to display. As the chariot passed a cliff, Deirdre was said to have leaned out and dashed her head against the rocks, ending her own life.

Deirdre was laid to rest in Emain Macha, close to the graves of Naoise and his brothers. In a final act of spite, Conchobar placed wooden stakes between the two lovers' graves, intending to separate them even after death. However, nature had its own plan. These stakes eventually took root and grew into two trees that intertwined, symbolizing the everlasting love between Deirdre and Naoise, a love that not even death nor the envy of a king could keep apart.

Thomas the Rhymer and the Queen of Elfland

While it is pretty common for love tales to end tragically, the story of Thomas the Rhymer and the Queen of Elfland breaks this mold in a captivating way. It is a tale not of sorrow and loss but of wonder, deep connection, and a love that transcends the boundaries of different worlds.

Some believe that Thomas the Rhymer was a real person, although it would be safer to call him a semi-legendary figure (a real person whose life story mainly lies in the realm of myth). He is said to have lived in the 13th century. His early life is shrouded in mystery, but it is safe to assume that he was just an ordinary man—at least before his encounter with the majestic Fae. This particular story began in the town of Erceldoune amidst the rolling hills close to the Scottish Borders. Thomas's heart yearned for the poetry of the natural world, and he often wandered the countryside. He could be seen by his fellow villagers taking a quiet stroll along the riverbed, his steps guided by the whispers of the wind and the peaceful songs of the streams.

On one fine day, perhaps slightly tired after exploring nature, Thomas found himself resting beneath an ancient tree. Its branches were heavy with blossoms—it was the beginning of spring. The tree was known by many as the Eildon Tree. Here, Thomas sat for hours. He was lost in his thoughts, his mind playing around with poetry and verse. It was then that Thomas suddenly felt a change in his surroundings. The air around Thomas shimmered with a strange, ethereal light, and the sound of silver bells danced upon the breeze.

Thomas the Rhymer and the Queen of Elfland's first encounter.
https://commons.wikimedia.org/wiki/File:Katherine_Cameron-Thomas_the_Rhymer.png

From the heart of this otherworldly glow emerged a vision that transcended the bounds of mortal comprehension. A horse, white as milk or even snow, bore upon its back a lady of such resplendent beauty that it seemed the very essence of the forest had taken form. Dressed in a gown of the deepest green and adorned with jewels that sparkled like dewdrops under the morning sun, she was a vision of enchantment. This was no mortal maiden but the Queen of Elfland herself.

Their eyes met, and in that gaze, a connection deeper than time itself was forged. Thomas was enraptured by her ethereal grace and felt his heart drawn to her as if by an invisible thread. The Queen, sensing the purity of his spirit, offered him a choice: journey into the unknown realms of Elfland in exchange for a kiss or do nothing and continue with his life, which would be forever unmarked by the wonders beyond. With a heart full of longing and a soul captivated by love, Thomas chose the path of the Fae. Without hesitation, he rose to his feet and kissed the otherworldly queen.

As soon as he made his choice, they journeyed to Elfland, a place where time moves differently. Days feel like years, and years pass in a moment. The Queen showed Thomas around this enchanting world, teaching him secrets and knowledge no mortal has ever known. Thomas was undoubtedly enchanted, as he was given a chance to see wonders beyond imagination—some he only heard when he was young in tales told by his elders.

However, fate and destiny had other plans for the two lovers. Their time together was bound by rules not of their making. Some claimed that every seven years, the fairies had to pay a tribute to darker forces. The Queen, fearing that Thomas might be the price of this grim levy, could not bear the thought of losing her beloved to such a fate. In a decision torn between love and duty, she chose to return him to the world of mortals.

Another tale spoke of a different reason for Thomas's return. It was said that the Queen, seeking to shield their love from the prying eyes of the Fairy King, sent Thomas back to Erceldoune. Their love was to remain hidden, a treasure known only to the hearts that bore it.

Whichever the reason, Thomas returned to the realm of humans under the same Eildon Tree. However, the Fairy Queen did not bid her goodbye without a gift. Thomas left the world of the Fae with a tongue that could not lie. Thomas could utter prophecies, and they would always be true. While some saw this ability as a blessing, others saw it as a burden.

Among his many predictions, Thomas foretold the death of King Alexander III, which led to the Wars of Scottish Independence. He spoke of a future where Scotland and England would unite under one crown, a prophecy realized centuries later with the accession of James VI of Scotland to the English throne. Thomas's visions extended beyond political realms, weaving tales of both love and loss.

Indeed, his gift brought him fame, but deep inside, he cherished the memories of Elfland and his time with the Queen more than anything. What happened to Thomas years later remains a mystery. Some say that Thomas was called back to the magical land and lives there still. Others believe he waits in secret, ready to return when Scotland needs him most.

Unlike other tragic love stories from that time, the tale of Thomas and the Queen did not end in sorrow. Instead, it lives on as a narrative of enduring love, magical adventure, and the idea that, even in a world steeped in tragedy, there can still be stories of wonder and hope.

Chapter 9: Sacred Sites

Much like its Celtic cousins—Ireland, Wales, and England—Scotland is home to various sacred sites. These sites are more than just monuments of stone and earth. They are also the silent witnesses to the land's colorful history and the still keepers of its deepest, mysterious, and enchanting secrets—be it of ancient kings, mythical creatures, or saintly miracles. From the enigmatic standing stones in the middle of nowhere to the hauntingly beautiful abbeys and eerie tombs, each site is a direct portal to a past that feels almost otherworldly. These places are important to properly understand Scotland's cultural identity, as they serve as reminders of a time when the natural world was revered and the veil between the earthly realm and the ethereal world was supposedly thin.

The Callanish Standing Stones

One of the most fascinating of these places is the Callanish Standing Stones. These towering stones, located on the Isle of Lewis in the Outer Hebrides, are a magnificent spectacle.

The history of the Callanish Stones is as deep and complex as the roots of the heather that blankets the Scottish moors. Erected around 2900 BCE, these megaliths predate Stonehenge. They are thought to have been placed by the hands of ancient people. The reasons why are lost to time, but the stones continue to fascinate us. However, for many centuries, the stones were concealed under a thick layer of peat turf and were only rediscovered in 1857.

The Callanish Stones during sunset.
Tom Richardson / Callanish at sunset:
https://commons.wikimedia.org/wiki/File:Callanish_at_sunset_-_geograph.org.uk_-_820680.jpg

The stones rise up against the skyline, tall and stoic. The standing stones measure at around twelve feet each and are arranged in a cruciform pattern around a central monolith of fourteen feet. They are made of Lewisian gneiss, a complex crystalline rock among the oldest in the world, dating back 1.7 to 3 billion years. These stones have witnessed numerous changing of skies and seasons. Some say this stone circle resembles an ancient gathering of wise men, forever locked in silent conversation.

The chambered tomb within the Callanish Standing Stones.
Nachosan, CC BY-SA 3.0 <https://creativecommons.org/licenses/by-sa/3.0>, via Wikimedia Commons: https://commons.wikimedia.org/wiki/File:Callanish_I_2011_17.JPG

The tales and myths surrounding the Callanish Standing Stones are as interesting as the stones themselves. One popular legend, capturing the mystical nature of the site, tells of the stones being petrified giants who refused to convert to Christianity and were punished by Saint Kieran. Another enchanting story involves a magical white cow with red ears that mysteriously emerged from the sea to provide milk to the islanders during a time of need. Sadly, the cow's kindness was cut short due to the greed of a particular visitor. The cow disappeared, never to be seen again.

According to archaeological findings, these stone formations were probably central to various rituals during the Bronze Age. Historians believe that the site was in use for at least a millennium before being abandoned around 1000 BCE. The most accepted theory today is that these megaliths functioned as an astronomical observatory or a calendar based on celestial events. It's believed that the arrangement of the stones aligns with the movement of the moon, particularly during the lunar standstill, which occurs every 18.6 years.

It is also widely believed that the stones were related to the agricultural calendar, perhaps marking important events like the solstice or the equinox. However, today, the site attracts those who seek a connection with the past or wish to celebrate ancient traditions. During solstices, people often gather on the site to watch the sunrise or sunset, with the sun aligning with the stones in a mesmerizing display of light and shadow.

The Isle of Iona

Nestled in the embrace of the Atlantic Ocean, right off the western coast of Scotland, lies a small yet profoundly significant isle known as Iona. This sacred island measures just three miles long and a mile wide. Iona is also so remote that the only way to reach this island from either Edinburgh or Glasgow is through a train ride, two ferry journeys, and a scenic bus ride. However, the island is often regarded as a beacon of spiritual and historical significance for centuries. Unlike the millennia-old Callanish Standing Stones, Iona's allure lies in its serene beauty and its rich Christian and Celtic history.

Iona's story begins in the mists of time, with its first inhabitants arriving in the late Neolithic era. However, the isle truly came into prominence in 563 CE with the arrival of Saint Columba from Ireland. Saint Columba, or Colum Cille, was not only a monk but also a noble and a poet. He established a monastic community on Iona, which soon became a center for the spread of Christianity throughout Scotland and beyond. The monastery he founded served as a religious center and as a seat of learning, attracting scholars and religious figures from across Europe.

Panoramic view of Iona.
https://commons.wikimedia.org/wiki/File:TvIona20030825r17f31.jpg

The island's monastery rapidly grew in fame and importance, becoming a renowned center for art and learning in the Celtic world. It was here that the famous Book of Kells, an illuminated manuscript containing the four Gospels of the New Testament, is believed to have been created by the monks of Iona in the 8th century. This masterpiece of Christian art showcases the deep spiritual and artistic heritage of the island.

Despite being a center of both learning and religion, Iona was not excluded from the violence of war. Throughout the centuries, Iona saw its own share of turbulence. It was once raided by the Vikings in 795 CE and then suffered several political power struggles. Nevertheless, the island remained a sacred site.

Of course, legends and tales also exist in Iona. The prominent one tells of Saint Columba's encounter with an angel on the island who showed him a vision of heaven. This encounter is said to have deeply affected the saint, influencing his teachings and writings.

Another story speaks of the "Street of the Dead," a path along which the bodies of kings and chieftains were carried to be laid to rest. It is also believed that Macbeth, the Scottish king made famous by Shakespeare, was buried here, along with many other rulers from Scotland, Ireland, and even Norway.

The Abbey on Iona.
User Karl Gruber on de.wikipedia, CC BY-SA 3.0 <http://creativecommons.org/licenses/by-sa/3.0/>, via Wikimedia Commons:
https://commons.wikimedia.org/wiki/File:Iona_Abbey_from_water.jpg

With its lush green hills that softly slope down to meet the soft, white sandy beaches and the vast expanse of the blue ocean, Iona offers a feeling of tranquility and reflection. The soothing sound of the waves and the calls of seabirds are usually the only things that disturb the profound quietness that surrounds the island.

As one walks the ancient paths of Iona, past the abbey and the ruins of a nunnery, there is a palpable sense of walking through history. The island is, more or less, a living museum, where each stone and every turn of the path tells a story of faith, art, and the enduring human spirit. It remains a place of pilgrimage, attracting those who seek solace, inspiration, and a deeper connection with the divine. To this day, the isle continues to be a shining jewel in Scotland's crown of sacred sites.

Arthur's Seat in Edinburgh

Believe it or not, Arthur's Seat, Edinburgh's most treasured mythic mountain, is actually an ancient volcano that last erupted about 340 million years ago. It has since eroded and glaciated to its current size. Standing at about 251 meters high, this extinct volcano gifts us with a panoramic view of the city and a journey into some of the most popular legends of Scotland. The history of Arthur's Seat is indeed as old as the rocks that form it, dating back hundreds of millions of years ago.

Arthur's Seat.
Kim Traynor, CC BY-SA 3.0 <https://creativecommons.org/licenses/by-sa/3.0>, via Wikimedia Commons: https://commons.wikimedia.org/wiki/File:Arthur%27s_Seat,_Edinburgh.JPG

However, how exactly the site got its name is shrouded in legend. Some say it is named after the legendary King Arthur, suggesting that it was one of the possible locations for Camelot, the legendary castle and court of the famous king. Others suggest that the dormant volcano had another name and that it was derived from a Gaelic phrase. Back when Holyrood Park was a royal hunting ground, an archer set a record for the longest arrow shot in the kingdom. His arrow was said to have flown an impressive 251 meters from the hunting area to the summit of the hill now known as Arthur's Seat. Since then, the locals started calling the hill "Àrd-na-Saighead" or "Height of Arrows" in recognition of this feat.

Arthur's Seat holds a few intriguing tales. One story tells us of a ferocious dragon known for terrorizing the old town of Edinburgh. Some say this tale predates even Celtic times. According to the age-old legend, the dragon never knew how to rest. Every day, the malicious creature would circle the sky, snatching and devouring any animals it came across, including the locals' livestock. The people of Edinburgh were beyond terrified of the dragon, especially when they did not know how to satisfy its never-ending greed. And so, the creature ate and plagued the humble lands continuously for years. However, in the end, it was its own greed that eventually led to the dragon's demise.

The dragon was believed to have grown extremely fat. Laziness took over the creature, and it no longer attacked the towns and villages. One day, the dragon flew to the hill just outside of Edinburgh. Perhaps exhausted from its daily excursions, the creature rested on the summit. Unfortunately for the gigantic dragon, that was the last time it ever flew again. As the legend goes, the dragon lay down to rest and fell into a deep slumber from which it never awoke. Over time, the dragon's massive body turned to stone, its curves and contours forming the hills and crags that now make up the landscape of Arthur's Seat.

Arthur's Seat is fascinating in regards to actual history as well. Archaeological finds, including a fort on the summit dating back to around 600 CE, suggest that it was an important site for early settlers. Perhaps the most intriguing mystery surrounding the extinct volcano emerged in 1836 with the discovery of miniature coffins.

A group of young boys were hunting for rabbits, and they stumbled upon a small cave on the northeastern slopes of Arthur's Seat. Inside this cave, they found something unexpected and startling: a collection of seventeen tiny coffins, each carefully carved and containing a small wooden figure dressed in custom-made clothes. The figures, which appeared to be dressed in a style resembling funeral attire, were meticulously crafted, with attention to detail that spoke of a deliberate and purposeful act.

The discovery of these miniature coffins set off a wave of speculation and theories about their origin and purpose. Some thought they were involved in witchcraft or were tokens to ward off evil spirits. Others speculated that they were connected to the infamous Burke and Hare murders, suggesting that the coffins represented each of the murderers' victims, though records claim that the murderers killed sixteen victims. This theory, though widely discussed, has little evidence to support it.

Another theory suggests that these coffins were created as a form of memorial, perhaps for sailors lost at sea. The attention to detail in the clothes and the careful arrangement of the coffins might indicate a grieving process or a tribute to the deceased.

The Clava Cairns

Near the banks of the River Nairn lies Clava Cairns, another site as mysterious as it is ancient. This complex of burial cairns and standing stones, dating back to the Bronze Age, about four thousand years ago, offers a fascinating glimpse into Scotland's prehistoric past. Unlike the vibrant tales of Arthur's Seat or the spiritual resonance of the Isle of Iona, Clava Cairns exudes an aura of ancient solemnity and profound mystique.

The Clava Cairns.
Nachosan, CC BY-SA 3.0 <https://creativecommons.org/licenses/by-sa/3.0>, via Wikimedia Commons: https://commons.wikimedia.org/wiki/File:Clava_cairn_(Balnauran_of_Clava)_28.JPG

Clava Cairns, also known as the Balnuaran of Clava, consists of a group of well-preserved burial cairns surrounded by standing stones. The site is divided into two types of cairns: passage cairns and ring cairns. The passage cairns, with their narrow passageways leading to central chambers, were likely used for burials, while the ring cairns, which have no apparent entrance, might have served a different ceremonial purpose.

The cairns are constructed with remarkable precision. Each one is surrounded by a circle of standing stones, with some stones positioned to align with the movements of the sun, particularly during the winter solstice. This alignment suggests that the site was not only a burial place but also a ceremonial space where ancient people might have celebrated and marked the changing of the seasons.

The stones themselves are a source of wonder. Made of a local variety of split stones known as whinstone, they range in height and shape, with some featuring mysterious cup and ring marks. These carvings might have held ritual significance; they were possibly used in ceremonies or as a way to mark ownership or heritage.

Legends and folklore are deeply entwined with Clava Cairns. One popular claim tells of spirits that guard the sacred site, protecting the ancient secrets buried within. Some even warned outsiders not to remain at the site during nighttime since the cairns hold mysteries that are beyond our mortal comprehension. About two decades ago, Clava Cairns was said to have inflicted a curse upon a Belgian tourist when he took a piece of a stone at the site as a souvenir. Little did he know, this tiny piece of memento brought havoc to his household, and he desperately sent the stone to a tourist office in Inverness, along with a letter explaining the incidents that had occurred. According to his writings, ever since he had brought the stone home, his family only knew misfortunes. His daughter broke her leg, his wife got mysteriously ill, and the man broke his arm and lost his job.

Mythic and peculiar incidents aside, the solitude and atmosphere of Clava Cairns are striking. Tucked away in a quiet grove, the site exudes a sense of uninterrupted time, offering a palpable connection to the distant past. Visitors often report a sense of awe and peace, as if stepping into a different world where time stands still and the modern world's noise fades away.

In recent years, Clava Cairns has gained international attention through its association with the popular *Outlander* series, as it inspired the fictional Craigh Na Dun, a place of time travel. This connection has brought new visitors who are eager to experience the mystical allure of the cairns for themselves.

The Whithorn Priory

The history of Whithorn Priory is deeply entwined with the spread of Christianity in Scotland. Founded around 397 CE by Saint Ninian, the first known Christian missionary to Scotland, the priory is considered one of the earliest centers of Christian worship in the country. Saint Ninian established a church at Whithorn, known as Candida Casa (White House), which allowed him to evangelize the surrounding regions. This church, the first stone-built church in Scotland, marked the beginning of a tradition of Christian worship and pilgrimage that has lasted for centuries.

Saint Ninian's chapel.
Ochoe at Dutch Wikipedia, CC BY-SA 3.0 <http://creativecommons.org/licenses/by-sa/3.0/>, via Wikimedia Commons: https://commons.wikimedia.org/wiki/File:Stninianschapel.jpg

The priory, whose ruins remain today, was established much later, around the 12th century. It became a site of significant religious and cultural importance, drawing pilgrims from across Scotland and beyond. The priory was home to a community of monks who followed the Premonstratensian order, which was known for its commitment to piety and learning.

Whithorn became a focal point for pilgrims, partly due to the belief that Saint Ninian was buried there. Pilgrims journeyed to the site, seeking spiritual solace, healing, and blessings. One prominent pilgrim was Robert the Bruce. In 1329, toward the end of his life and suffering from a serious illness, Robert the Bruce made a pilgrimage to Whithorn. He sought healing and perhaps divine favor at the shrine of Saint Ninian. Despite his faith and the hope for a miracle, Robert the Bruce succumbed to his illness three months after his visit.

Whithorn Priory, the nave of the cathedral.

Otter, CC BY-SA 3.0 <http://creativecommons.org/licenses/by-sa/3.0/>, via Wikimedia Commons: https://commons.wikimedia.org/wiki/File:Whithorn_Priory_20080423_nave.jpg

David II, Robert the Bruce's son, also made an important pilgrimage to Whithorn. Legend says that during the Battle of Neville's Cross in 1346, David II was hit by two arrows. One of these arrows could not be removed. However, after a pilgrimage to Whithorn's shrine, the arrow was finally taken out successfully.

The significance of Whithorn Priory extends beyond its religious history. It was a center of learning and culture, with monks playing a vital role in the preservation and production of religious texts and artifacts. Today, the site's ruins, including the Priory Church, offer a glimpse into its grand past.

Whithorn has also seen a revival of pilgrimage in recent years. The Whithorn Way, a modern pilgrimage route, allows visitors to follow in the footsteps of medieval pilgrims, journeying through the stunning landscapes of southwestern Scotland to the historic site. This contemporary pilgrimage experience connects people with the rich spiritual heritage of Whithorn, blending past and present in a journey of reflection and discovery.

Conclusion

As we travel through the misty highlands and deep lochs of Scotland's mythological landscape, we are constantly reminded of the profound influence these ancient tales hold in shaping the nation's culture, identity, and storytelling tradition. This book has been a voyage across time, delving into a variety of tales, characters, and themes. These stories are not only central to Scottish mythology but have also continued to resonate deeply with modern audiences, both young and old alike.

Scottish mythology's continued appeal lies in its ability to speak to the human condition and to explore the depths of our fears, desires, and hopes. These ancient stories remind us of our connection to the past, to the land, and to the shared human experiences that transcend time and place. They are more than just tales; they are a window into the soul of a nation, reflecting the values, beliefs, and aspirations of the Scottish people.

The lasting impact of Scotland's mythological heritage is clear in modern culture, arts, and literature. These ancient narratives, filled with heroism, romance, tragedy, and the supernatural, have stood the test of time, inspiring numerous creative works. In films and television shows, elements of Scottish myths are often woven into narratives, creating worlds filled with magic and wonder. For instance, the allure of the Scottish Highlands, haunted by the spirits of its past and the legends of its people, has captivated filmmakers, leading to cinematic portrayals that paint the nation's myths and history in a new light.

In literature, the influence of Scottish mythology is equally profound. Novels, both historical and fantasy, frequently draw upon the rich well of Celtic lore, reimagining old tales or embedding mythological themes within new stories. Characters like the 13th-century Scottish leader William Wallace, mythical creatures such as kelpies and the Loch Ness Monster, and historical events, such as the witch hunts, have found new life in pages and screens, enchanting a new generation of readers and viewers worldwide.

Music, too, has been touched by these ancient narratives. Traditional Scottish music often encapsulates the essence of these myths, with ballads telling tales of love, loss, and adventure. Contemporary musicians continue to draw inspiration from these stories, using them to create songs that speak of the land's ancient past and the timeless human experiences reflected in these myths.

The reinterpretation of classic legends and the incorporation of mythological themes in new works are not just acts of creativity; they're proof of the lasting importance of these stories. They serve as bridges connecting the past with the present, keeping the essence of Scottish mythology vibrant in our shared awareness.

As we look to the future, there is hope that these captivating stories will continue to be cherished, shared, and reimagined. It is essential that Scotland's mythological wisdom, values, and heritage remain a vital part of the nation's cultural legacy. In a world that is rapidly changing, these myths offer a link to the past, grounding us in tradition while inspiring new stories and interpretations.

If you enjoyed this book, a review on Amazon would be greatly appreciated because it would mean a lot to hear from you.

To leave a review:
1. Open your camera app.
2. Point your mobile device at the QR code.
3. The review page will appear in your web browser.

Thanks for your support!

Here's another book by Enthralling History that you might like

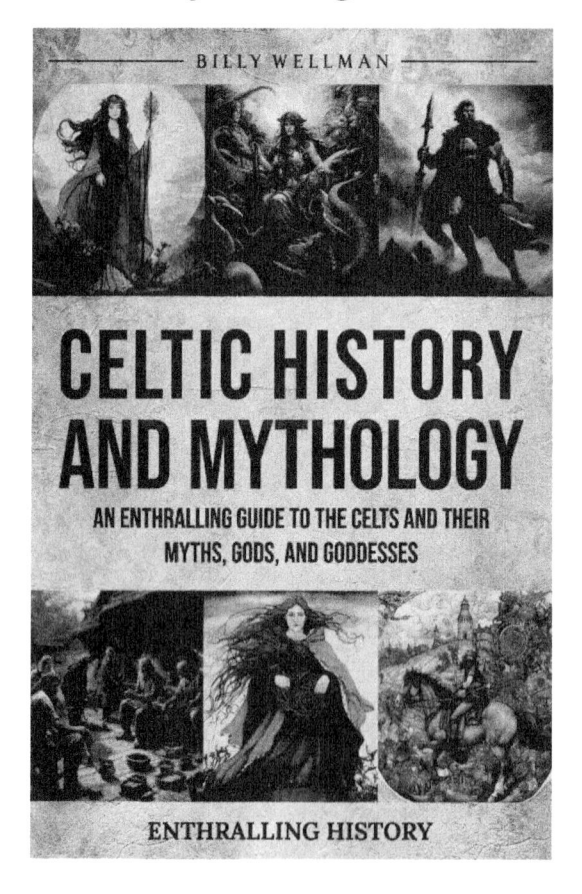

Free limited time bonus

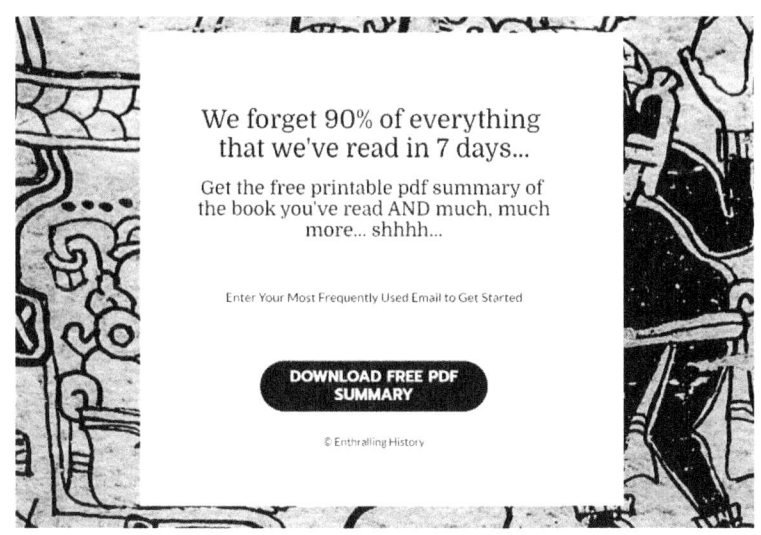

> We forget 90% of everything that we've read in 7 days...
>
> Get the free printable pdf summary of the book you've read AND much, much more... shhhh...
>
> Enter Your Most Frequently Used Email to Get Started
>
> **DOWNLOAD FREE PDF SUMMARY**
>
> © Enthralling History

Stop for a moment. We have a free bonus set up for you. The problem is this: we forget 90% of everything that we read after 7 days. Crazy fact, right? Here's the solution: we've created a printable, 1-page pdf summary for this book that you're reading now. All you have to do to get your free pdf summary is to go to the following website: **https://livetolearn.lpages.co/enthrallinghistory/**

Or, Scan the QR code!

Once you do, it will be intuitive. Enjoy, and thank you!

Bibliography

Brown, C. (2022, May 18). The Callanish Standing Stones: Stonehenge of the North. Good Nature Travel Blog | Stories Are Made on Adventures. https://www.nathab.com/blog/callanish-standing-stones/

Brown, R. (2023, April 5). The Two Sisters and the Curse. Folklore Scotland. https://folklorescotland.com/the-two-sisters-and-the-curse/

By The Newsroom. (2016, April 19). Five parts of Scotland you didn't know were cursed. The Scotsman. https://www.scotsman.com/whats-on/arts-and-entertainment/five-parts-of-scotland-you-didnt-know-were-cursed-1478389

By The Newsroom. (2016, April 19). Five parts of Scotland you didn't know were cursed. The Scotsman. https://www.scotsman.com/whats-on/arts-and-entertainment/five-parts-of-scotland-you-didnt-know-were-cursed-1478389

By The Newsroom. (2016, October 25). Was tourist cursed by sacred Highland site? The Scotsman. https://www.scotsman.com/whats-on/arts-and-entertainment/was-tourist-cursed-by-sacred-highland-site-613927

Cameron, E. (2019, March 6). Legends of Argyll — Eilidh Cameron Photography. Eilidh Cameron Photography. https://www.eilidhcameronphotography.com/blog/2019/3/6/legends-of-argyll

Cartwright, M. (2023). Lugh. World History Encyclopedia. https://www.worldhistory.org/Lugh/#google_vignette

Deirdre of the Sorrows – Bard Mythologies. (n.d.). https://bardmythologies.com/deirdre-of-the-sorrows/

Facts, legend & History | Callanish (Calanais) Standing Stones. (2023, December 18). Calanais. https://calanais.org/explore/

Fairnie, R. (2019, October 29). Bone-chilling story behind Craigleith house "haunted" by ancient Egyptian mummy. Edinburgh Live. https://www.edinburghlive.co.uk/news/edinburgh-news/bone-chilling-story-behind-craigleith-17162657

Graeme. (2023, November 21). Scottish Witch Stories: The Facts & The Fiction. Scotland's Stories. https://scotlands-stories.com/scottish-witch-stories/

Great Castles - Lady Ghosts of Crathes Castle. (n.d.). https://great-castles.com/crathesghost.html

Great Castles - Lady Ghosts of Crathes Castle. (n.d.). https://great-castles.com/crathesghost.html

Hale, R. (2023, August 7). Hermitage Castle, Scotland's Fortress Of Nightmares | Spooky Isles. Spooky Isles. https://www.spookyisles.com/hermitage-castle/#google_vignette

Haunted Rooms. (2023, January 31). The Ghosts of Mary King's Close, Edinburgh | Haunted Rooms. Haunted Rooms. https://www.hauntedrooms.co.uk/mary-kings-close

IrishCentral Staff. (2023, March 21). The legendary "Deirdre of the Sorrows" and the Celtic tale's legacy. IrishCentral.com. https://www.irishcentral.com/roots/legendary-deirdre-sorrows+

Jackcairney. (2022, July 7). Legends from the Old Man of Storr - Hidden Scotland. Hidden Scotland. https://hiddenscotland.co/legends-from-the-old-man-of-storr/#:~:text=Some%20say%20the%20Old%20Man,their%20long%20and%20happy%20marriage

Jackcairney. (2022, July 7). Legends from the Old Man of Storr - Hidden Scotland. Hidden Scotland. https://hiddenscotland.co/legends-from-the-old-man-of-storr/

Jewelry, S. I. (2023, May 5). The Legend of the Selkies: A Love & Transformation story. ShanOre Irish Jewelry. https://www.shanore.com/blog/the-legend-of-the-selkies/

Kingshill, S., & Westwood, J. (2009). The Lore of Scotland: A guide to Scottish legends. https://openlibrary.org/books/OL25081911M/The_lore_of_Scotland

Mark, J. J. (2023). Clava Cairns. World History Encyclopedia. https://www.worldhistory.org/Clava_Cairns/#google_vignette

Pilgrimage. (n.d.). https://www.whithorn.com/origins/pilgrimage/

Scott, & Scott. (2023, March 14). What is Scottish Witchcraft (or not)? – the role of the wise women. The Cailleach's Herbarium. https://theCailleachs-herbarium.com/2015/09/what-is-scottish-witchcraft-or-not-the-role-of-the-wise-women/#:~:text=Witchcraft%20in%20Scotland%20was%20known,to%20a%20%E2%80%9Cfoolish%20women%E2%80%9D

Scottish legends: The Cu Sith. (n.d.). Folkrealm Studies. https://folkrealmstudies.weebly.com/scottish-legends-the-cu-sith.html#google_vignette

Smith, K. (2019, April 3). 10 of the most wicked witches in Scottish history. Scottish Field. https://www.scottishfield.co.uk/culture/10-of-the-most-wicked-witches-in-scottish-history/

St. Ninian. (n.d.). https://www.whithorn.com/origins/st-ninian/

The horrifying execution of William Wallace. (n.d.). Mercat Tours Ltd, Edinburgh, Scotland. https://www.mercattours.com/blog-post/the-horrifying-execution-of-william-wallace

The Kelpie, mythical Scottish water horse. (2017, August 26). Historic UK. https://www.historic-uk.com/CultureUK/The-Kelpie/

The mystery of the miniature coffins. (n.d.). National Museums Scotland. https://www.nms.ac.uk/explore-our-collections/stories/scottish-history-and-archaeology/mystery-of-the-miniature-coffins/

The mystery of the miniature coffins. (n.d.). National Museums Scotland. https://www.nms.ac.uk/explore-our-collections/stories/scottish-history-and-archaeology/mystery-of-the-miniature-coffins/

Printed in Great Britain
by Amazon